"Words can't express how thankful I am for this curriculum As a former middle school Bible teacher, I know how impossible it is to find truly gospel-c̶ ̶ ̶ ̶ ̶ ̶ ̶ ̶ ̶ ̶ ̶ ̶ ̶ in a format that young people can process . . . and will find interesti̶ ̶ ̶ culture awash with moralistic messages and frilly sillines̶ ̶ od news written for young minds. Seriously, I can't recomm̶ ̶ ̶ "

Elyse Fitzpatrick, Author of *Good News for Weary Wor̶ ̶ *

"What an amazing gift, *What's Up?* is going to be for middle-school anu junior ̶ ̶ ̶ and parents of fifth through eighth-graders. Debbie Harrell and Jack Klumpenhower have done an outstanding job of contextualizing the gospel of God's grace for kids in one of the most vulnerable for formative seasons of life. I get excited just thinking about how this curriculum, in the hands of grace-loving leaders, will help disciple a new generation of gospel-equipped, Jesus-loving students. And let me add, the teachers are going to benefit just as much as the students. Great job, Debbie and Jack. More, more, more!"

Dr. Scotty Ward Smith, Founding Pastor of Christ Community Church; Teacher in Residence at West End Community Church; author of *Everyday Prayers: 365 Days to a Gospel-Centered Faith*

"Have you ever wondered how you could explain the great truths of the gospel to your children? *What's Up?* takes you step by step with solid teaching, thoughtful questions, insights, and practical application—always leading you to Christ. It is a must-read for parents, teachers, young and old."

Rose Marie Miller, Author of *From Fear to Freedom* and *Nothing Is Impossible with God*

"If you read Jack Klumpenhower's book, *Show Them Jesus*, but didn't think you could teach as well as Jack does—don't worry. The *What's Up?* curriculum and teacher's guide give you everything you need to teach your middle school students the same amazing gospel lessons Jack presented in his book. You'll have parents thanking you for the amazing way their kids are learning deep gospel truths like justification, adoption, how to recognize false repentance, and how to offer true forgiveness. It doesn't matter what curriculum you are currently using with your middle school, put it on hold and get your kids through this material—that is what I am going to do at my church."

Marty Machowski, Family Life Pastor and author of *Long Story Short* and *Old Story New*, *The Gospel Story Bible*, the *Gospel Story for Kids* curriculum and *Prepare Him Room*

"Preteens can be critics. It's just part of how we grow at that age. Deborah and Jack know the best way to fight a critical spirit—a clear vision of Jesus, an honest assessment of our hearts, and a faithful commitment to working out the implications of the gospel in our relationships. *What's Up?* is a clear and engaging tool for applying these truths to middle school kids."

Jared Kennedy, Pastor of Families, Sojourn Community Church, Louisville, KY

"I love this study! Deborah Harrell and Jack Klumpenhower have done a fine job at communicating gospel-saturated truth for students and have given teachers a reliable and easy-to-use guide. *What's Up?* is a helpful tool to faithfully plant and water the gospel of Jesus Christ in the hearts of students. If you are looking for a biblical, Christ-centered, and holistic study for teenagers, look no further!"

Brian H. Cosby, Author of *Giving Up Gimmicks: Reclaiming Youth Ministry from an Entertainment Culture* and *Rebels Rescued: A Student's Guide to Reformed Theology*; pastor and visiting professor at Reformed Theological Seminary

"Congratulations to Deborah and Jack for taking on the most challenging group of all—our kids. In *What's Up?* they attempt to teach young people both the gospel and how to live out of the gospel. Why wait until we get locked into a pattern of performing or pretending? Why not be discipled in the gospel from the beginning? That is what these creative and engaging lessons do and do well."

Stephen Smallman, Assistant Pastor, New Life Presbyterian Church, Glenside, PA; author of *The Walk-Steps for New and Renewed Followers of Jesus*

"Harrell and Klumpenhower's *What's Up?* middle school curriculum beautifully lives up to its subtitle: *Discovering the Gospel, Jesus, and Who You REALLY Are*. I love its thoroughness, flexibility, and teaching style. More importantly, its model of student discipleship (believe—don't just try harder) coupled with the practical 'make-it-stick' section packs a powerful gospel-driven one-two punch. It should be required curriculum for all youth ministries!"

John C. Kwasny, PhD, Director, *One Story Ministries*

"*What's Up?* is a curriculum that will challenge both students and teachers to delve deep into the definition, meaning, and significance of Christianity. It encourages students to look squarely into their hearts and discover whether or not they are truly living for themselves or for their Creator."

Susan Wall, Children's Ministry Curriculum Coordinator, Capitol Hill Baptist Church, Washington, DC

WHAT'S UP?

Discovering the Gospel, Jesus, and Who You REALLY Are

Deborah Harrell and Jack Klumpenhower

New Growth Press

WWW.NEWGROWTHPRESS.COM

Cover/Interior Design and Typesetting Matthew Bomberger
ISBN 978-1-939946-72-0

Printed in the United States of America

22 21 20 19 18 17 16 15   2 3 4 5 6

TABLE OF CONTENTS

UNIT ONE: THE GOSPEL

UNIT TWO: YOUR HEART

UNIT THREE: A CHANGED LIFE

Dear Parent,

Welcome to *What's Up? Discovering the Gospel, Jesus, and Who You Really Are.* This study is designed for middle school (5th–8th grade) students. It encourages them to believe the good news of Jesus and live it out.

We are grateful for the opportunity to partner with you in the discipleship of your child. *What's Up?* is designed for a group study and each lesson builds on the others. If your child misses a session, he or she can complete the missed lesson at home, but may need some parental guidance and support. Likewise, if your child wants to do *What's Up?* individually, you (or some other adult mentor) should become the "group" and review the lessons alongside your child.

In either case, if you think you will be guiding your child through some lessons, you should obtain a leader's edition of *What's Up?* The *Teacher Guide* contains instructions and explanations that help you through the lessons and activities. The *Teacher Guide* also gives detailed explanations of what your child will be learning and how the group sessions are conducted. Even if you don't plan on leading your child through any of the lessons, having your own copy may help you follow up on the teaching at home without having to look through your child's student workbook, which may contain private reflections.

You may find that *What's Up?* challenges your child to live as a believer in ways he or she has seldom considered before. There will be Make It Stick assignments for home that require prayer, Bible reading, discussions with others about Jesus, and more—often on a daily basis. Your support and encouragement will be important if your child is to get the maximum benefit from these assignments. It may help to ask your child about these assignments during the week or to remind him or her to bring the *Student Guide* to each class.

Our prayer is that throughout the *What's Up?* study you and your child's love for Jesus will grow. May God bless and encourage you as you study together.

Blessings in Christ,
Debbie and Jack

INTRODUCTION

IS *WHAT'S UP?* FOR ME?

Yes, it's for you if you want to learn more about Jesus or grow in your life with him. Maybe you only know a little bit about the Bible, and want to learn what believing in Jesus means. *What's Up?* will teach you what it's all about—and show you how to get started, if that's what you decide. Or maybe you've heard and read the Bible so much that you know every story by heart, but now you want to live it out. *What's Up?* will help you look to Jesus and delight in all he's done for you—and believe!

BUT WHAT IF I ALREADY BELIEVE?

That's great! But faith must always grow. You know that you often fail to be kind in how you treat your friends, classmates, parents, and teachers. *What's Up?* will teach you not to hide or ignore that sin, but to admit it and trust Jesus. You'll learn to enjoy how he always forgives you. You'll believe more deeply that he died for you and made you God's holy, ever-welcomed child. You'll learn to live the way someone who believes those things ought to live. That's growing in faith!

WILL IT MAKE ANY DIFFERENCE IN MY LIFE?

Oh, if you come to know you're God's child, it makes *all* the difference. It gives you love for your Father so you want to live for him. You'll see how much he cares for you and for *everything* you do, so that you become excited about life with Jesus. It also gives you confidence that God is on your side—even when you fail! You can stop being scared of God when you've sinned and instead go to him for help. You'll not only learn to resist sin that way; you'll learn to constantly trust and live close to Jesus. *What's Up?* won't just change how you think as a child of God. It should also change how you *act* as a child of God.

WHAT WILL I BE DOING?

You'll work through your lesson pages with a Bible and a pen or pencil. *What's Up?* will guide you as you rely on God to help your faith grow. You'll spend much time using the tools *he* gives you to help you learn. Here's what you'll use:

The Bible. God speaks to you through the Bible. These lessons will use the Bible to teach you and will get you reading your Bible.

Prayer. Prayer is how you talk to God and ask him for help. Since you need God's help to grow, the lessons and assignments in *What's Up?* will include lots of prayer.

The good news of Jesus. Jesus and all he does for us are the main message of the Bible, so *What's Up?* will keep mentioning this good news again and again. You need to keep remembering and believing it.

Other believers. God makes believers in Jesus part of his family so they can help each other grow more faithful. These lessons will get you sharing with a group, talking about your faith with others, and learning from an experienced leader.

WHAT IF I DON'T HAVE A GROUP?

The lessons are designed for group study. Sharing with others in a group will be the best way for you to learn the most from *What's Up?* If you don't have a group, you can still do the study by yourself, but even then you need to find an adult leader to be your mentor and guide you through the lessons. That person will be who you share with—and will also share *their* stories with *you*. This kind of sharing is an important part of *What's Up?*

WHAT WILL THE LESSONS BE LIKE?

Most lessons will have three segments:

BEFORE YOU BEGIN. Since *What's Up?* is about your whole life— not just lesson time—you'll start by talking about your life! You share what you've learned and how you've been practicing faith since the last time your group met.

TODAY'S LESSON. Lesson time will include several discussion and workbook pages. *What's Up?* keeps you doing stuff all through the lesson. You'll be writing and drawing on your lesson pages: underlining, doodling, matching, writing answers, and drawing pictures—that kind of thing. You'll also read from the Bible, discuss the lesson with your group, and pray.

Important note: You might think discussing your faith and praying is TOO HARD. Try it anyway. It gets easier with practice, and it's an important part of Christian growth.

MORE important note: You might think underlining, circling, and writing answers on your lesson pages is TOO EASY. Do it anyway. Of course it's easy, but it's the best way for you to notice what you're learning—like taking notes. (Besides, you get to write, draw, and doodle on your lessons, which is sweet!)

MAKE IT STICK. Here you'll get directions for practicing what you learned during the week. It's important to always do the Make It Stick assignment during the week. It's what makes *What's Up?* about your whole life. Plus, you'll be reporting how it went the next time you meet with your group. Even though Make It Stick is something you'll do at home on your own, it's still a group activity that'll end up helping the whole group when you discuss it together later.

ANOTHER important note: Make It Stick is *practice*. *What's Up?* is a discipleship course. It trains you in how to live. That's why daily practice, and sharing with your group how it went, is so important.

WHAT ELSE SHOULD I EXPECT?

Expect God to work in you. He loves you. Jesus died on the cross to save all who believe in him. "He gave his life to free us from every kind of sin, to cleanse us, and to make us his very own people, totally committed to doing good deeds" (Titus 2:14 NLT). Start praying now that God will use *What's Up?* to help make everything that verse says true of *you*. God is determined that his people will grow. Look forward to it.

LESSON 1

OH... NOW I SEE

Big Idea: Seeing Jesus

BEFORE YOU BEGIN

In these lessons, you're going to learn about God from the Bible. Maybe you're wondering: what are the basic facts about who God is?

- Use the God Fact Sheet to get you started. To keep it fun, do this:
- Check off things you already knew about God. (✔)
- Put a star next to things you might have heard before, but weren't sure about.
- Write "wow!" next to anything that's brand new to you. *WOW!*

THE GOD FACT SHEET

ONE God. There is only one God. He's a spiritual being, and he created *everything* that exists.

- ☐ God is eternal. He was never created. He has always existed and always will exist.
- ☐ God is all-powerful. He knows and controls everything.
- ☐ God is holy. He's perfect and pure of any evil, which he calls "sin." He never sins and can't stand sin.

THREE persons. Even though God is only one, he exists as three persons—the Father, the Son, and the Holy Spirit. Each person is *all the way* God (eternal Creator, all-powerful, perfect, and holy). These three persons . . .

- ☐ Communicate with each other.
- ☐ Make agreements with each other (they never disagree, because God is one).
- ☐ Love each other (perfectly, of course).

Our Savior. The three persons work together in everything, including acting together to save us from our sin. They each have a special role in saving us.

- ☐ The Father lovingly ordered our salvation and sent the Son to be our Savior.
- ☐ The Son accomplished our salvation by taking the punishment that we deserved for our sin.
- ☐ The Holy Spirit changes us so we can be saved by believing that the Son died for us. He also teaches us to resist sin and live for God.

Jesus. To be our Savior, about 2,000 years ago the Son became a human being—without stopping to still be *all the way* God too. He was born and took the name Jesus. Jesus is both God and also *all the way* a man! As a man, there are things about him that ordinarily wouldn't be true of God.

- ☐ Jesus got tired, hungry, and thirsty. He also has every human emotion (but only in non-sinning ways, since he's still holy God).
- ☐ Jesus was tempted to sin, like we are (but he never did sin).
- ☐ Jesus suffered and died before being raised to life again.

Now tell the rest of the group what you learned from the God Fact Sheet. What was really interesting to you? Was anything confusing?

Let's do one thing more. Before starting these lessons you probably already have an idea about what Christianity is. So think of a word or short phrase that describes being a Christian and then tell what you wrote.

Christianity is _____.

TODAY'S LESSON

In this lesson, you'll learn a word *Jesus* chose to describe what he's all about. First, you'll learn what this word is. You'll also get a "clear vision" view of why it makes being a Christian different from what many people think.

Then, in the second part of this lesson, you'll compare that word to other ideas and feelings you might have about God—"blurry vision" ones.

PART 1: EXACTLY THE RIGHT WORD

When Jesus lived on earth, he picked a word to explain what his work was all about. He chose the word "gospel." It means "good news." In those days, no one had ever used that word for religion! It was used for good news brought by a king's messenger—like news of a battle won. It was news everyone would be glad to hear and let change their life. Our Bibles sometimes use the word "gospel" and sometimes say "good news," but they're the same thing.

 Point to remember: "Gospel" means GOOD NEWS!

Let's see what the Bible says about this good news.

You may have heard about the angel who told shepherds about baby Jesus. That angel was being a messenger, bringing good news—the gospel!

> And the angel said to them, "Fear not, for behold, I bring you good news of great joy that will be for all the people. For unto you is born this day in the city of David a Savior, who is Christ the Lord." (Luke 2:10–11)

Find "good news" in those verses and (circle) it.

Then find the word "Savior" and put a star ★ next to it.
Finally, underline the part of the angel's message that tells WHOM the gospel is all about.

The missionary Paul wrote about the gospel in the Bible. Read what he said.

Now I would remind you, brothers, of the gospel I preached to you, which you received, in which you stand, and by which you are being saved, if you hold fast to the word I preached to you—unless you believed in vain.

For I delivered to you as of first importance what I also received: that Christ died for our sins in accordance with the Scriptures, that he was buried, that he was raised on the third day in accordance with the Scriptures. (1 Corinthians 15:1–4)

Again, ⟨circle⟩ **the word "gospel."**

Find the part where Paul says the gospel is about being saved and put a star by it. ★
And <u>underline</u> the sentence that tells WHOM the gospel is about and what he did for us.

The gospel is news about the Christ (that's a title for JESUS). It's about how he SAVES US.

You're ready to start filling in your "clear vision" view of the gospel. Start by writing WHOM the gospel is about on the blank eyeglass lens that follows.

Now fill in WHAT Jesus does for us in the gospel. (Hint: It's what you put the stars by in our verses.)

TALK ABOUT IT

Most of the time, do you feel like you need Jesus to save you from anything? Why or why not? When do you most feel like you need a Savior?

Remember that "sin" means we do evil things that are against God. We deserve to be punished.

Find Romans 3:23–24 in your Bible. Read it to learn more about what it means to be saved. Then write an answer to the question below.

HOW are we saved from sin? Is it because we earn *it* by being good and not sinning, or is it a *gift* God gives us through Jesus? Fill in the eyeglasses with your answer.

Now read one more Bible verse that tells about being saved. Look up John 3:16 and answer the two questions below.

WHY did God decide to give his Son, Jesus, to save us? HOW do you respond in order to have eternal life?

Believing in Jesus includes:

- **Trusting Jesus** instead of trying to be good enough to save yourself.
- **Living for Jesus** and obeying him instead of living for yourself.

Now use your answers to fill in the last parts of your gospel vision. Start by writing WHY God saves us, as a gift, through Jesus.

Finally, write what you do to respond to this good news.

★ THE ★ GOSPEL

HOW do I respond?

Now let's combine what you've learned about the gospel with what you know about God:

GOD IS HOLY. He hates sin. Since you're a sinner who does wrong every day, you need to be saved from sin to be accepted by a holy God.

GOD IS FAIR. He punishes sin. Sinners must die. So *you* must be punished unless <u>someone else</u> who's perfectly good takes your place as a substitute.

GOD IS LOVING. He gave his Son, Jesus, to be that <u>someone else</u>. Jesus was punished instead of you—in your place!—if you believe in him. This means you can be accepted by God even though you sin.

TALK ABOUT IT

Discuss the three points listed above. Which do you most often hear people talk about? Which are new to you or are ideas you don't think about much? Explain why *all three* are important.

TEST YOURSELF

Circle the believer in each pair of students who has "clear vision" of the gospel, and tell why.

GOOD NEWS

"Christianity is mostly about what I have to do for God."

"Christianity is first of all about good news of what God does for me!"

WHY?_____

_____

_____

SIN

"I'm a far worse sinner than I thought. I offend the holy God so often! No matter how hard I try, I can't make myself good enough for him."

"As long as I try hard to be good, God shouldn't think of me as too bad a sinner."

WHY?_____

_____

★ ACCEPTED ★

"God accepts me whenever I'm good like I should be, and he gets grumpy with me when I'm not."

"God accepts me because Jesus is good, and I belong to Jesus. He took the punishment I deserve."

WHY?_____

JESUS

"Jesus loves me. He died for me! Now I obey him because he means everything to me."

"I need to obey Jesus better if I want him to like me."

WHY?_____

BELIEVE IT!

"Believing in Jesus means that now I both trust him and live for him eagerly, every day. It changes everything!"

"Believing in Jesus means I can go on with my life and hardly have to think about my sin anymore. I'm glad it's so easy and doesn't require much change!"

WHY?_____

PART 2: BLURRY VISION

Seeing the gospel clearly is like an eye exam. Even if you already know about the gospel, sometimes your vision can get "blurry." So now, *you be the eye doctor*. For each student, find what that student <u>can't see</u> about the gospel.

Maybe it's . . .

- ☑ What a big sinner they are
- ☑ How God accepts them because of Jesus, not how good or bad they are
- ☑ How Jesus loves them and died for their sin
- ☑ How believing the gospel means a new, changed life

Then, once that student has a "prescription" to see the gospel more clearly, describe how you think their life will change.

THE SMUG STUDENT

"Sometimes I sin, but I'm better than most people. I study the Bible and I obey at school; and I'm sure God has noticed. There are bad people who need Jesus much worse than I do. God is glad that I'm one of the good guys!"

BLURRY VISION

This student <u>can't see</u> (check what applies):

- ☐ They're a big sinner just like everyone else.
- ☐ God accepts them because of Jesus, not how good they are.
- ☐ Jesus loves them and died for their sin.
- ☐ Believing in Jesus means a new, changed life.

PRESCRIPTION

THE GOSPEL SAYS: You're a big sinner too. God only accepts you because of Jesus, not how good you think you are.

LIFE WITH GOSPEL VISION

When you see the gospel, you'll stop bragging and being proud. You'll quit trying to prove how good you are. Instead, you'll . . .

_____

_____

_____

THE NERVOUS STUDENT

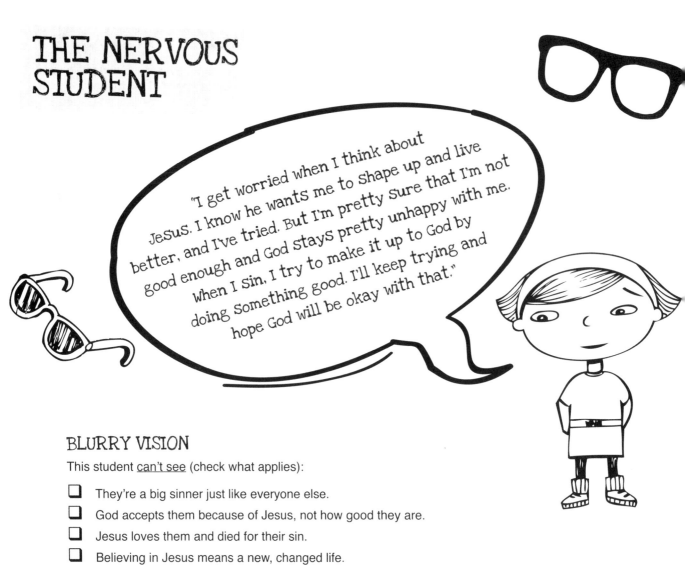

"I get worried when I think about Jesus. I know he wants me to shape up and live better, and I've tried. But I'm pretty sure that I'm not good enough and God stays pretty unhappy with me. When I sin, I try to make it up to God by doing something good. I'll keep trying and hope God will be okay with that."

BLURRY VISION

This student <u>can't see</u> (check what applies):

- ☐ They're a big sinner just like everyone else.
- ☐ God accepts them because of Jesus, not how good they are.
- ☐ Jesus loves them and died for their sin.
- ☐ Believing in Jesus means a new, changed life.

PRESCRIPTION

THE GOSPEL SAYS: You don't have to earn your forgiveness. God accepts you because of Jesus. It's free!

LIFE WITH GOSPEL VISION

When you see the gospel, you'll stop worrying and being secretly scared of God. You'll quit doing good things only because you feel pressure. Instead, you'll . . .

_____

_____ .

THE ALL ABOUT ME STUDENT

"I just LOVE doing good things at church and with Christian friends. It's fun to help out, be part of youth events, and work on projects that make the world better. Everyone says I'm doing great and I feel good about that. I don't know if I'm really doing those things for Jesus, but I sure enjoy them!"

BLURRY VISION

This student <u>can't see</u> (check what applies):

- ☐ They're a big sinner just like everyone else.
- ☐ God accepts them because of Jesus, not how good they are.
- ☐ Jesus loves them and died for their sin.
- ☐ Believing in Jesus means a new, changed life.

PRESCRIPTION

THE GOSPEL SAYS: Jesus died for you. He loves you *that* much! *He's* the best reason to serve God.

LIFE WITH GOSPEL VISION

When you see the gospel, you'll stop doing godly-looking things just because they're fun, or because people are watching. Instead, you'll . . .

_____

_____

_____ .

THE EASY LIFE STUDENT

"I sin quite a bit, but I don't worry about it. God forgives me, like he's supposed to. Pretty easy, huh? I guess I appreciate Jesus for that. But I don't understand people who say they love to worship him and pray or change their life for him. That's never happened to me."

BLURRY VISION

This student <u>can't see</u> (check what applies):

- ☐ They're a big sinner just like everyone else.
- ☐ God accepts them because of Jesus, not how good they are.
- ☐ Jesus loves them and died for their sin.
- ☐ Believing in Jesus means a new, changed life.

PRESCRIPTION

THE GOSPEL SAYS: Believing in Jesus means your life isn't about yourself anymore. You don't trust yourself. You don't live for yourself, either. You change so that you trust and live for Jesus, instead.

 ## LIFE WITH GOSPEL VISION

When you see the gospel, you'll no longer have a self-centered life that finds Jesus boring. Instead, you'll . . .

_____

_____

_____ .

BLURRY GOSPEL VISION

Which blurry vision student are you most like?

THE SMUG ONE

"Yes, sometimes I sin, but I'm better than most people. I do Bible studies and I obey at school, and I'm sure God has noticed. There are bad people who need Jesus much worse than I do."

YOU CAN'T SEE

You're a big sinner—much worse than you think!—especially in how you look down on others.

GOSPEL PRESCRIPTION

You're a big sinner just like everyone else. God only accepts anyone because of Jesus, never because of how good they are.

Your life with GOSPEL vision:

You stop being proud and start to treasure Jesus. It's he who gives you a good reputation with God, so you no longer feel a need to prove how good you are. You stop bragging and learn to care about others.

THE NERVOUS ONE

"I don't always admit it, but I'm secretly worried that I'm not good enough for God. When I sin, I try to make it up to God by doing something good. I'll keep trying and hope God's okay with that."

YOU CAN'T SEE

God loves and accepts you even though you still sin.

GOSPEL PRESCRIPTION

God loves you even though you still sin. Jesus took your place. You don't have to earn your forgiveness. It's free!

Your life with GOSPEL vision:

You stop feeling worried and learn to rest in God's love. This lets you love God back instead of being scared of him. You start to do good things eagerly— out of thankfulness, not due to pressure.

THE ALL ABOUT ME ONE

"I just LOVE doing good things at church and with my friends. It's fun to be part of youth events and to do things that make the world better. Everyone says I'm doing great—so I guess I am!"

YOU CAN'T SEE

Jesus has died for you. You're just doing good things because you enjoy them and they make you feel good about yourself—not really for Jesus.

GOSPEL PRESCRIPTION

Jesus died for you. He loves you *that* much!

Your life with GOSPEL vision:

The reason why you enjoy doing good things changes. You start to do them because you're glad to be repenting— Changing your life out of love for Jesus. You're eager to serve him even when it isn't fun and you live for him even when no one is watching.

THE EASY LIFE ONE

"I don't worry about my sin. God forgives me, like he's supposed to. Pretty easy, huh? I appreciate Jesus for that, but I don't understand people who say they love to worship him and pray. That's never happened to me."

YOU CAN'T SEE

The gospel must change everything about how you live. It's bigger than cheap forgiveness.

GOSPEL PRESCRIPTION

Your sin was not easy to fix and the change Jesus brings is huge. He *died* to give you *new life*. Now the Spirit makes you able to live for him—and to love it!

Your life with GOSPEL vision:

You're thankful to Jesus and eager to fully enjoy your new life with him. You pray often, trusting the Spirit to help you grow. Since Jesus is all-important to you, worshiping him is not boring.

Looking at the Blurry Gospel Vision figure, think about each student with "blurry vision." Which one is most like *you*? Once you pick which one you're most like, circle it, and share your choice with the group. Explain how your way of thinking about God is sometimes like that blurry vision.

PRAY ABOUT IT

Remember how the Holy Spirit helps us believe the gospel? Everyone needs clearer gospel vision—even people who've believed the gospel for many years! So now, ask God to help you. Pray with a friend or by yourself. Here's how to do it:

Look back at the type of blurry vision you circled. Then look at the final box labeled "your life with gospel vision."

Pray for the things written in that box to happen to you. Pray that the Holy Spirit will change you so that those things become true of you as you learn and believe the gospel through these lessons.

You can either say your prayer aloud or write it out in a few sentences below.

_____

_____

_____

_____

_____.

NOTE: As you learned what believing the gospel means, you may have thought to yourself: "Hmm, I'm not sure I've ever actually believed the gospel." If that's the case with you, consider becoming a believer. You can start believing (by trusting Jesus to save you and deciding to live for him) at any time—the sooner the better! But as you've learned, it's an important decision that you need to consider carefully and take seriously. The rest of our lessons will help you learn more about what it means to be a believer.

The rest of the lessons will also speak to you as if you already *are* a believer. Those who believe in Jesus are forgiven, have become God's children, have eternal life—and more! These lessons will help believers to believe these things more deeply, so they can grow. If you actually aren't a believer yet, you too can learn about Jesus and all he does for us. Our hope is that you will come to believe for the first time—and then keep believing more deeply all your life.

MAKE IT STICK:

GET TO KNOW JESUS

INSTRUCTIONS:

Fill out this Make It Stick page during the week.

Don't forget to bring your *Student Guide* back next time you meet.

If you have time, go ahead and get started now.

Jesus isn't just a way to be forgiven and accepted by God. He's also a person—the *best* person you could ever know! So before the next time you meet, practice getting to know Jesus better by reading about him in the Bible and noticing what kind of man he is.

Start by reading **Luke 7:11–17**. It's a short account of a time when Jesus visited a town called Nain. Read what happened there.

Then, on the lines below, write words or short phrases that tell what kind of person Jesus is—based on just this one, short story. Look closely at the details in the story and fill out as many lines as you can. It might help to consider these questions:

What abilities does he have?
How does he treat people?
What does he feel?
What are his attitudes?
What surprises you about his behavior?
How is he different from you?

(You don't have to answer each question. Just use them to help you think of some words that describe Jesus.)

_____

_____

_____

_____

_____

_____

Be ready to share what you noticed about Jesus the next time you meet.

THAT'S MY WHOLE LIFE STORY

Big Idea: The Gospel Story

BEFORE YOU BEGIN

Remember what you learned last time. Jesus brought the GOSPEL. It means GOOD NEWS.

Look back to the start of Lesson 1. What was the word you wrote down to describe Christianity near the beginning of that lesson? How does the gospel compare to the word you picked?

Jesus is both our Savior (one who saves us from sin) and an amazing person. Share what you learned about him from reading Luke 7:11–17. What are some of the words you used to describe him?

What do you think is the *most amazing* thing about the kind of person Jesus is—the thing that most makes you want to know him better and live your life for him?

TODAY'S LESSON

Don't you just love a great story, one you can't put down!

Imagine a character in such a story is in a life or death situation. They can't get out on their own. They need a hero to rescue them.

As you read you suddenly realize that character is <u>you</u>! You can't get out on your own. You need a hero. The story you're reading is the true story of how Jesus called you to believe in him, to rescue <u>you</u>.

Jesus is the main character in the big, true story told in the whole Bible. Plus, he's *your* Savior if you believe in him. In this lesson, you'll learn his story— the story of how we've sinned and are saved by Jesus. It's your story too.

Let's take the story chapter by chapter, like in one of those picture storybooks you had when you were a kid. (If you're working in a group, it'll probably work best to read each section of the story and fill in the blanks together.)

CHAPTER 1: GOD'S PERFECT WORLD

Everything began with God—Father, Son and Holy Spirit—each person loving and honoring the others. His creation was like him, perfect and without the slightest sin. God filled the world with his beauty and his glory. From the first twinkling star to the massive whales that navigate the oceans, all of God's creation was good. People were most special of all.

God created man in his own image, in the image of God he created him; male and female he created them. (Genesis 1:27)

"Everyone who is called by my name, whom I created for my glory, whom I formed and made." (Isaiah 43:7)

What do the Bible passages say people were like when God created them?

_____

_____

What does Isaiah 43:7 say people were created for?

_____

It is easy to read the creation story and think, "This has nothing to do with me. It happened long before I was even born." But read what the Bible says about how *you* were part of that story too, way back in the beginning.

[God] chose us in him before the foundation of the world, that we should be holy and blameless before him. (Ephesians 1:4)

Put on the new self, created after the likeness of God in true righteousness and holiness. (Ephesians 4:24)

God chose you to be in this story and planned to rescue you. You too are created to glorify him and enjoy him forever—to be with him and be like him, holy and blameless.

So to remind yourself that God created you to be LIKE HIM and WITH HIM, <u>add yourself to the story by drawing a picture of yourself in the creation picture above</u>. Then fill in the blanks below.

"God created me in his own

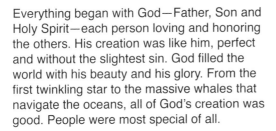

to be _____.

My purpose is to

_____ him."

TALK ABOUT IT

Share how it feels to know *you* were created to be like God, holy and caring for others.

"God sure loves others, doesn't he?"

"And we're made to be like him. That makes what comes next pretty bad."

CHAPTER 2: REBELLION

The first man and woman, Adam and Eve, lived in God's perfect world. But the devil came (as a serpent) and tempted them to eat from the one tree God had commanded them not to eat from. They disobeyed God.

Their selfish rebellion made them God's enemies. It doomed them to live apart from God and to die that way, with sinful and evil hearts. They deserved for God to destroy them.

> When the woman saw that the tree was good for food, and that it was a delight to the eyes, and that the tree was to be desired to make one wise, she took of its fruit and ate, and also gave some to her husband who was with her, and he ate. (Genesis 3:6)
>
> The wrath of God is revealed from heaven against all ungodliness and unrighteousness of men. (Romans 1:18)

God had told Adam and Eve not to eat the fruit. Underline the three reasons why Eve decided to eat it anyway.

Was she loving God? Or was she being selfish, thinking about what she could get for herself?

In the passage above, circle the words that tell what selfish, sinful people deserve.

Now you may be asking, "Why do I get punished for something someone else did? That's SOOOOO not fair!" But sadly, the sin Adam did and the evil that took over his heart is spread to every person, including you.

> Sin came into the world through one man, and death through sin, and so death spread to all men because all sinned. (Romans 5:12)
>
> No one does good, not even one. (Romans 3:12)

So add to the picture above to show that you've been selfish and sinned too. Draw a picture of yourself in the picture. Then fill in the blanks below.

"I am a

_____,

just like Adam and Eve. I deserve

_____

as a punishment."

TALK ABOUT IT

What do you think of how Adam's sin spread to everyone, including you? Do you sense this is true of you? Does it seem right and fair?

CHAPTER 3: THE GOSPEL

God loved the world so much that he saved his enemies. The Son, Jesus, became a human being. He obeyed the Father perfectly, but took the horrible punishment guilty people deserve. Jesus was nailed to a cross to bleed and die in a shameful and cursed way. On that cross, he died in place of everyone who believes in him.

Jesus was buried, but came back to life in victory! Now the devil is doomed. Jesus rules from heaven and will return one day to judge all people and to live forever with those who believe.

> *For God so loved the world, that he gave his only Son, that whoever believes in him should not perish but have eternal life. (John 3:16)*
>
> *Christ also suffered once for sins, the righteous for the unrighteous, that he might bring us to God. (1 Peter 3:18)*
>
> *The reason the Son of God appeared was to destroy the works of the devil. (1 John 3:8)*

In these verses, underline all the amazing, good things that come to sinners who believe in Jesus.

What happens to the devil's evil works because of Jesus?

_____

Here's the best part of the story, the part where you are rescued from death—yes, death! If you believe in Jesus, you are *joined to him* forever. He died—so your sin died too! He came alive—so you do too! He's with God in heaven—so you will be also!

> *We know that our old self was crucified with him in order that the body of sin might be brought to nothing, so that we would no longer be enslaved to sin. (Romans 6:5–6)*
>
> *[God] raised us up with him and seated us with him in the heavenly places in Christ Jesus (Ephesians 2:6).*

So <u>draw a picture of yourself in the picture of the cross and empty tomb</u>. Know that you are part of this story! You're joined to Jesus. The stuck-in-sin person you used to be is dead. Jesus has given you a new life that lets you love God, and one day he will give you a new, never-dying body too. Now fill in the blanks below.

"My old self was _____ with Jesus, so I'm not trapped in sin anymore.

God has _____ me to new life with Jesus."

TALK ABOUT IT

Have you ever thought about these things before:

❏ That when Jesus died, you died too (in a way)?

❏ That when Jesus rose from the dead, you became alive too (in a way)?

❏ That as Jesus rules from heaven, you're with him there (in a way)?

How might knowing you're *that closely* joined to Jesus change how you think and act?

"So we all sinned because of Adam, but we have new life because of Jesus."

"THAT IS GOOD NEWS!"

CHAPTER 4: YOUR LIFE TODAY

Now believers are no longer God's enemies. Instead, they're his dearly loved children. God has given them salvation and changed their hearts. They look to Jesus as they live in this world, knowing they have a mighty Father who will help them when they struggle with selfishness and sin. They learn to love, like their Father, as they wait for Jesus's return.

> *For the grace of God has appeared, bringing salvation for all people, training us to renounce ungodliness and worldly passions, and to live self-controlled, upright, and godly lives in the present age. (Titus 2:11–12)*

In these verses, our salvation (being saved) is called "grace." That means we didn't earn it and don't deserve it. We got it from Jesus. What two things does God's grace teach us to renounce (give up)?

_____

_____

What are three words that describe believers' lives when they know God's grace?

_____

_____

_____

This time, draw the entire picture of yourself in the story. Think of a time when you were tempted to do something wrong—something disobedient, dishonest, or selfish. Draw a picture of yourself saying "no" to that sin, like a believer should, or draw a picture of yourself loving someone else the way Jesus has loved you. That's your life today if you believe in Jesus! YOU are still part of the story.

As children of God who are joined to Jesus, the Bible tells us to "consider yourselves dead to sin and alive in Christ Jesus" (Romans 6:11). Being joined to Jesus means *we keep dying every day!* Some ways you might "die" to sin and selfishness are:

You give up trying to get your own way all the time. Example from your life:

_____

_____

_____

You give up insisting you be first. Example from

your life:_____

_____

_____

You stop complaining when you have to obey someone else. Example from your life:

_____

_____

You love your neighbor like you love yourself. Example from your life: _____

_____

"This part of dying with Jesus doesn't sound like good news. It sounds like it's no fun."

"Are you sure? Think about it. How might dying to yourself and all your selfishness be a good thing that actually brings you joy?"

TALK ABOUT IT

From the list above, pick one or two ways you might die to yourself. On the lines, write examples from your life of how you would do that. Share what you wrote with the group.

Doing those things feels hard, doesn't it? It sounds like death! Well, *of course it does*. But discuss how becoming less concerned about yourself might also be sweet. How might it give you deeper joy? How might dying to yourself also be the way to a new, greater, sweeter life?

MAKE IT STICK:
WATCH YOUR WORDS

INSTRUCTIONS:

☐ Fill out this Make It Stick page during the week.

The gospel tells us that Jesus makes us good in God's eyes. Believing this should help us no longer feel a need to make ourselves look good to others, either by bragging about ourselves or putting other people down. James 3:2 says, "If anyone does not stumble in what he says, he is a perfect man."

This week, practice living like God's child by watching your words (what you say).
For one week, or until the next time you meet, do not:

- Lie

- Say unkind things about others (gossip)

- Put anyone down

- Complain

- Brag

- Hide your sin

- Make excuses

- Defend yourself (even if you're wrongly accused)

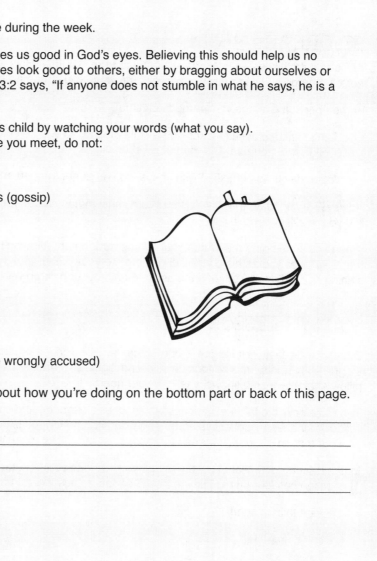

If you like, you can keep notes about how you're doing on the bottom part or back of this page.

_____

_____

_____

_____

MY TONGUE IS CONNECTED TO MY—WHAT? Big Idea: Sin of the Heart

BEFORE YOU BEGIN

Talk about the Watch Your Words assignment from last time. How well did you do? What parts of it were the hardest? List or discuss some of the ways you struggled.

Remember some things you learned last time:

- Being joined to Jesus makes you a child of God, so you can love him and obey him gladly—even in how you use your tongue.

- Your old self was crucified with Jesus, so you're not trapped in sin anymore.

However, trying to do the Watch Your Words assignment under your own power might make you *feel* like you're still trapped in sin.

When you were doing the Watch Your Words assignment, did you think to believe the gospel—that God loves you as his child? Did you pray to your Father and trust him to help you keep from sinning? Or did you try to keep the assignment in your own power?

TODAY'S LESSON

Did you know that your tongue is one of the hardest working organs in your body? Not only is your tongue busy talking, mixing food, swallowing, fighting germs, and keeping you from drooling on your pillow at night—it also shows what's in your heart.

The Bible says the tongue can deceive, lie, gossip, slander, and speak hatred. It can also speak wisdom, kindness, gentleness, truth, and worship. The tongue is powerful! And the things we say with our tongue show us our need for the gospel every day (even every minute).

In this lesson, you'll learn how the things you *say* with your tongue show what you *love* in your heart. The lesson has four steps. They're based on four things you might want to say along the way:

- "I want to look right!"

- "Don't blame me!"

- "I'm not so bad deep down . . . am I?"

- "So what hope do I have?"

"I WANT TO LOOK RIGHT!"

You may never be tempted to steal. You may not struggle with cheating on a test. So why is controlling your tongue different? Why was the Watch Your Words assignment SO HARD?

Read Matthew 6:1. Fill in the blanks to see something all of us naturally want—but Jesus said we should beware of.

"Beware of practicing your _____ before other

people in order to be _____" (Matthew 6:1).

Controlling your tongue is so hard because we want to look right to other people. We want others to think we're . . .

good . . .

or smart . . .

or fun to be with.

We want this SO MUCH that we'll sin with our tongues to try to make it happen. We'll lie and brag and say bad things about others.

Let's look at how we try to make ourselves look right to others. Match each behavior from the Watch Your Words assignment with the I-want-to-look-right *motives* for doing them. Write the tongue behavior beneath the motive. (Some behaviors might fit more than one motive.)

1. Lying
2. Gossiping
3. Putting people down
4. Making excuses
5. Bragging
6. Complaining
7. Defending yourself
8. Hiding your sin

"I'm sure to point out anything I do right in case others missed it. I whine if they don't agree."

"I make other people look bad so I'll look better."

"When I'm wrong, I try to keep anyone from noticing or I make up a story about being right."

"I can't handle it when others think I'm wrong, so I always correct them."

TALK ABOUT IT

Now tell about how *you* want to look right to other people. What are some places and times in your life when looking right to others feels especially important to you? Give an example of how you sometimes sin with your tongue to try to make yourself look right in those situations.

God makes us right in his eyes when we have faith in Jesus. That's the kind of "being right" we really need! Wanting to make ourselves *look* right to others is the wrong kind of "being right." It's called "self-justification."

Self-justification: Trying to make yourself look right or not guilty.

Self-justification happens *very* easily. It's like a reflex—like how you hold up your hand to protect yourself if you're about to be hit. In the same way, when we're caught doing wrong our reflex action is to deny it or blame someone else (even if that hurts the other person!).

Let's look at some examples in the Bible.

Look up and read: Genesis 3:8–12. It's about when Adam and Eve were caught disobeying God.

When Adam was caught doing wrong, did he admit his sin or try to make excuses and blame someone else?

_____

Who did he blame?

_____

Look up and read: Exodus 32:21–24. It's about when Moses caught Aaron in sin after Aaron made a golden calf for the people to worship.

When Aaron was caught doing wrong, did he admit his sin or try to make excuses and blame someone else?

_____

Who did he blame?

_____

What excuses, and even lies, did he come up with?

_____

TALK ABOUT IT

Now think of a time (either during the Watch Your Words assignment or some other time) when you were caught doing wrong and made excuses or blamed someone else. Tell about it. How were you trying to make yourself look right instead of admitting your sin?

"I'M NOT SO BAD DEEP DOWN . . . AM I?"

The urge to defend yourself is so strong it can cause you to say all sorts of evil or even silly things, like how Aaron claimed the calf just came out of the fire. Those sinful things you say come from deep down.
Read what Jesus said about them:

"A good man brings good things out of the good stored up in his heart, and an evil man brings evil things out of the evil stored up in his heart. For the mouth speaks what the heart is full of." (Luke 6:45 NIV)

According to Jesus, where do the things you say come from?

_____

Whatever <u>attitude</u> you took toward the Watch Your Words assignment came from your heart too. Check which attitudes you felt.

I worked hard at the assignment because of . . .

☐ <u>Spiritual pride</u>. I wanted to prove how godly I am.

☐ <u>Duty</u>. It seemed like the right thing for a Christian to try.

☐ <u>Need to please</u>. Not doing it or doing poorly would have disappointed God, others, or myself.

I tried to avoid the assignment because of . . .

☐ <u>Resentment</u>. I didn't like having an "assignment" tell me how I should behave.

☐ <u>Fear</u>. I was worried about how poorly I might do and who might find out.

☐ <u>Discouragement</u>. It seemed too hard.

☐ <u>Stubborn pride</u>. I didn't want to admit it might be good for me or teach me something.

I mostly ignored the assignment or forgot about it because of . . .

☐ <u>Not caring</u>. Other things were more on my mind.

☐ <u>Coldness</u>. Living in a godly way just doesn't get me excited or hold my interest.

TALK ABOUT IT

Discuss the attitudes you checked. What has the Watch Your Words assignment taught you about your sin? How deep does the sin go?

"SO WHAT HOPE DO I HAVE?"

Let's review. Think of and list three things you've learned in this lesson about how you sin with your tongue.

_____

_____

_____

_____

_____

You might think this sounds like horribly **BAD NEWS!**

But it's actually part of the **GOOD NEWS**—the gospel. These are three reasons why you need Jesus!

By now you should realize that <u>you're a far worse sinner than you ever thought</u>. This means you can give up trying to fight your sin by yourself. It'll never work. Trust Jesus instead. Only Jesus can change a sinful heart!

 Point to remember:
When you fight to not sin, don't try to do it by yourself.
Do it by trusting God.

No matter how yucky your sin is (and it's VERY yucky!), God forgives you when you believe in Jesus. And no matter how much evil is in your heart, God still loves you and helps your heart change.

A godly king named David wrote Psalm 139. It's a prayer in the Bible. David understood how God knew all his secret sins yet loved him anyway. Here's part of the prayer he wrote:

Search me, God, and know my heart; test me and know my anxious thoughts. See if there is any offensive way in me, and lead me in the way everlasting. (Psalm 139:23–24 NIV)

David's prayer asks God for six things. Find them and list them below.

1. _____

2. _____

3. _____

4. _____

5. _____

6. _____

Look at the list. First <u>underline</u> any words that mention something that gets in the way of enjoying God.

Now put a star next to every request that invites God to know or see something about us—even our sin!

Now add another star next to the part that asks God to change us.

PRAY ABOUT IT

Finally, make David's prayer your prayer too. Trust God and invite him to know the truth about your heart and to change you. Have each person in the group pick two of the requests that have stars next to them. Take turns praying that God would do those things in your life, or write out your prayer below.

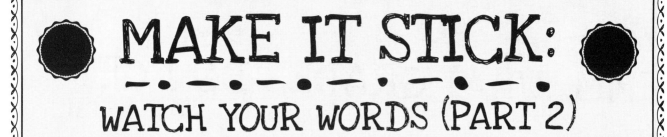

MAKE IT STICK:
WATCH YOUR WORDS (PART 2)

INSTRUCTIONS:

❑ Fill out this Make It Stick page during the week

The Watch Your Words assignment was hard, wasn't it? Well, God is so holy and good that his commands about the tongue are actually *even harder* than that. It isn't enough to AVOID saying bad or selfish things. There are also good and kind things we DO say.

Ephesians 4:29 (NIV) says, "Do not let any unwholesome talk come out of your mouths, but only what is helpful for building others up according to their needs, that it may benefit whose who listen."

This week, focus on what you DO say. Talk in ways that benefit others. Instead of trying to make yourself look good, admit your mistakes and confess your sin. Instead of bragging about yourself, talk lots about how good others are. Especially, talk lots about the goodness of Jesus.

Until the next time you meet, do the following:

·   Admit your mistakes

·   Confess your sin to others

·   Tell others you're sorry when you hurt them (and mean it!)

·   Encourage others (this includes not getting jealous if they do something better than you, but instead congratulating them)

·   Give good reports about others

·   Tell others about Jesus

Again, you can keep notes on this page if you like.

LESSON 4

HMM...WHAT GRADES DO I GET?

Big Idea: Justification by Faith

BEFORE YOU BEGIN

How did you do with the second part of the Watch Your Words assignment? This time,
give yourself a grade (from A to F) on how well you controlled your tongue in each of these areas:

ASSIGNMENT	GRADE
Admitted your mistakes (without being asked)	-------------
Confessed your sin to others	-------------
Told others you were sorry when you hurt them	-------------
Encouraged others and congratulated them when they did better than you	-------------
Gave good reports about others	-------------
Told others about Jesus	-------------

Discuss the grades you gave yourself and share some examples of what you did to deserve your
grades.

TODAY'S LESSON

Last time, you learned how tempting it is to try *self-justification*.
Find the definition of self-justification from the last lesson and write it here:

_____

Today's lesson is about how you can look right <u>to God</u>. Instead of self-justification,
you'll learn about a better kind of justification that comes from God. It's called *justification by faith*.

"WHAT'S SO BAD ABOUT TRYING TO PROVE TO GOD HOW GOOD I AM?"

One day Jesus told a story to a crowd of self-justifiers. The story was about two men. First learn about the characters in his story:

Pharisee

Respected member of a synagogue (like a church)

Worked hard at carefully obeying God's laws

Known by all to be a good person

Tax Collector

Traitor who worked for the Romans—the enemy!

Got rich by taking other people's money

Known by all to be a bad person

Now read Jesus's story in **Luke 18:9–14**.

Pick and write two things the Pharisee told God about himself.

One bad thing he was NOT: _____

One good thing he did: _____

Do you see? The Pharisee was a good person in many ways, but he was still wrong because he was trying to justify himself before God! He was trying to make himself look right and not guilty to God. That never works if you really want to be *justified*.

 Justification: When God says he counts you righteous, not guilty.

"SO IF JUSTIFICATION COMES FROM GOD, HOW DO I GET IT?"

Let's start with how good or bad you are. Give yourself grades again. This time, imagine God keeps a report card on *all* your behavior— not just "tongue" behaviors. Put your name on the report card. Then fill in the grades you think your life has earned from God, from A to F. Try to be honest.

Report Card

Telling the truth ☐

Encouraging others ☐

Obeying parents ☐

Being generous ☐

Putting others first ☐

Name:

TALK ABOUT IT

Now discuss the grades you gave yourself. What have you done to earn them? Do you think you're doing okay, or are you concerned that your grades aren't better?

If you're either proud of your grades or worried about them, it means you're trusting *yourself* instead of Jesus. You're a self-justifier.

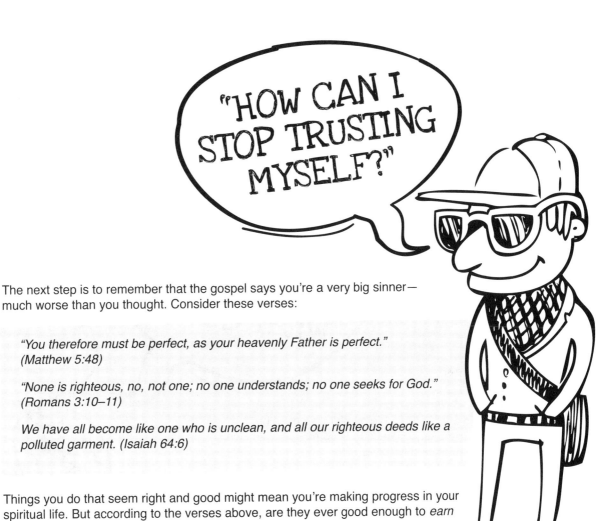

The next step is to remember that the gospel says you're a very big sinner— much worse than you thought. Consider these verses:

> *"You therefore must be perfect, as your heavenly Father is perfect."* (Matthew 5:48)

> *"None is righteous, no, not one; no one understands; no one seeks for God."* (Romans 3:10–11)

> *We have all become like one who is unclean, and all our righteous deeds like a polluted garment. (Isaiah 64:6)*

Things you do that seem right and good might mean you're making progress in your spiritual life. But according to the verses above, are they ever good enough to *earn* anything from God?

_____

Report Card

Telling the truth ☐

Encouraging others ☐

Obeying parents ☐

Being generous ☐

Putting others first ☐

Name:

In school, you get an okay grade even if your work is not perfect. But God is so holy that he demands PERFECT grades! With God, anything not absolutely perfect earns an F.

Adjust your report card to fit the way God sees your attempts to impress him by yourself. Write your name on it again. This time give yourself all Fs. That's the only grade you've *earned* from God.

"HOW CAN I IMPROVE MY GRADES WITH GOD?"

Having all Fs with God is a big problem because he demands straight As. You need to become right with God. You need a report card full of As.

1. THE "A FOR EFFORT" SOLUTION:

"If I try real hard to be good, God might decide trying was good enough."

"WON'T WORK. You'll end up awfully discouraged and worried. You'll soon realize you can never try hard enough."

Quickly draw a worried face here.

2. THE "FORGIVENESS ONLY" SOLUTION:

"God forgives, doesn't he? I can ask him to just erase all my Fs."

"WON'T WORK. That isn't good enough. You'll be left with just a blank report card. Your Christian life will feel like a burden as you try to earn some As to get God to not just forgive you, but actually like you."

Draw a frustrated face here.

3. THE "CREDIT FOR NOTHING" SOLUTION:

"WON'T WORK. What good is an A that hasn't been earned? You'll never appreciate it because it's so cheap."

"God can just give me all As. He's nice and he can do anything."

Draw an I-don't-care face here.

Which false solution is most like the way you sometimes think about your sin problem? Circle 1, 2, or 3. Discuss why these solutions are false ones.

Now here's God's solution for making you right with him. Write your name again on the first report card—the one with all Fs. Now notice there's a second report card. It belongs to Jesus!

The Bible says Jesus "has been tempted as we are, yet without sin" (Hebrews 4:15). Think of all the perfectly good things Jesus did. Then mark Jesus's report card with all A+'s for his good life.

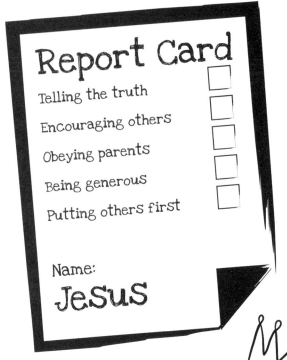

 Justification: What makes one right in God's eyes

Now read some verses that tell us God's solution—how we become *justified* and *right*.

For our sake he made him to be sin who knew no sin, so that in him we might become the righteousness of God. (2 Corinthians 5:21)

Who actually sinned? (Circle) one   Me   Jesus
But who gets punished for it? (Circle) one   Me   Jesus
Who actually did right? (Circle) one   Me   Jesus
But who gets righteousness? (Circle) one   Me   Jesus

For Christ also suffered once for sins, the righteous for the unrighteous, that he might bring us to God. (1 Peter 3:18)

Who was right, but still suffered?

_____

Who was not right, but still gets to be accepted by God?

_____

The righteousness of God has been manifested . . . through faith in Jesus Christ for all who believe . . . and are justified by his grace as a gift. (Romans 3:21–24)

Where do we get this righteousness?

_____

Do we earn it by anything we do?

_____

If not, how *do* we get it?

_____

When you belong to Jesus by believing in him, it's like he's traded report cards with you.

- ❑ <u>Jesus took your sin</u>. By dying on the cross he took the punishment for everything wrong you've ever done or will do. He suffered the anger of God that you deserve and all the shame of being wrong.

- ❑ <u>God gives you Jesus's right record</u>. God no longer sees you as shameful and wrong. Instead he sees the righteousness of Jesus when he looks at you and all you do. You are forever justified.

Now turn back to the last set of report cards. On Jesus's report card scratch out his name. Write YOUR NAME in its place. This is now *your* report card. Then scratch out your name on the bad report card and write "Jesus" in its place.

TALK ABOUT IT

Share how it felt to do this. Were you embarrassed back when you had to give yourself the Fs? How does it feel now to know Jesus took that shame for you?

How does the unearned righteousness God gives you feel different from the kind of right reputation you have to earn?

Becoming right with God doesn't happen because of anything good you do. You get it by placing your **faith** in Jesus. You stop trusting what *you* do and start trusting *him*, instead.

Faith: Believing that Jesus died for your sin and trusting him—not your own good behavior— to make you right with God.

PRAY ABOUT IT

End by saying a prayer.

- ❑ Pray that the Holy Spirit would free you from the need to prove yourself.

- ❑ Pray that he would teach you to trust the perfect righteousness that comes from Jesus, instead.

- ❑ Pray that you'll stop being either proud or worried.

Speak your prayer aloud or write it below.

_____

_____

_____

_____

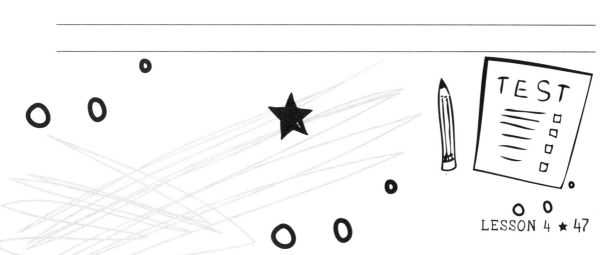

MAKE IT STICK:

TEACH JUSTIFICATION BY FAITH

INSTRUCTIONS:

- ❑ Fill out this Make It Stick page during the week.

- ❑ If you have time, go ahead and get started now.

Now it's *your* turn to teach someone else how we become right with God. Pick someone and teach it to them before the next time you meet. That's when you'll report to the group on how it went.

You may pick someone who already knows all about justification or someone who doesn't. It's your choice. (Just don't be bossy, like *they* need to hear it. Explain that you're doing it because it helps *you* learn.)

Study first. You can learn about justification from the three verses you read near the end of this lesson: 2 Corinthians 5:21; 1 Peter 3:18; and Romans 3:21–24. When you teach, you may also use the report card illustration if you want. Make sure your teaching includes these five points:

1. We are sinners; we are not right with God.

2. Jesus, who was perfect, took the punishment we deserve.

3. We become right with God by trusting Jesus in faith, not by anything good we do.

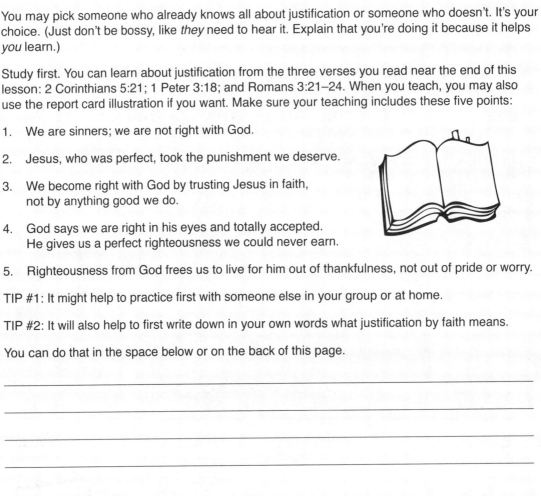

4. God says we are right in his eyes and totally accepted. He gives us a perfect righteousness we could never earn.

5. Righteousness from God frees us to live for him out of thankfulness, not out of pride or worry.

TIP #1: It might help to practice first with someone else in your group or at home.

TIP #2: It will also help to first write down in your own words what justification by faith means.

You can do that in the space below or on the back of this page.

_____

_____

_____

_____

LESSON 5

PRESENTS? FOR ME?!

Big Idea: Holiness and Fighting Sin

BEFORE YOU BEGIN

Talk about how it went teaching justification by faith. You should have taught five things:

1. **Sin** – We are not right with God.

2. **Jesus** – He did right, but took the punishment we deserve.

3. **Faith** – We become right with God by faith in Jesus, not by anything good we do.

4. **Righteousness** – God says we are right in his eyes and totally accepted. He gives us a perfect righteousness we could never earn.

5. **Freedom** – The great thing about righteousness from God is it frees us to live for him out of thankfulness, not because we're worried or proud.

Did you do the assignment? If so, did you talk about Jesus happily or did you wish you didn't have to?

Sometimes people get scared to talk about Jesus because . . .

❑ They think they won't say things right, or . . .

❑ It feels too personal, or . . .

❑ They worry what others will think of them.

Did you get scared in any of those ways? Which ones?

When it happened, did you remember that your righteousness comes from Jesus—not how well you do or what others think of you?

TODAY'S LESSON

Justification is great! But in this lesson you'll learn how it's only the start. God also gives you other, equally stunning gifts when you believe in Jesus—like getting presents. All these presents will make you more confident when you have to do hard things for Jesus (like tell people about him).

PART 1: PRESENTS FROM GOD

In this section you'll learn about the presents God gives you.
You'll also think about what makes them great.

REVIEW:

In Lesson 2, you learned that when you believe in Jesus your life is *joined to him*.

❑   Like he was killed, your old sinful life is dead.

❑   Like he was raised to life, you have a new life now.

Think of being joined to Jesus as a birthday—one where you get lots of presents. You might open the first gift and it's *so* good that you think, "Wow! This present has to be the BIG ONE!" But then you open more and find that the other presents are just as awesome.

Now let's learn about three of the great presents believers get from God. The first is one you already know about . . .

GOD'S PRESENT FOR YOU: JUSTIFICATION

Joined to Jesus, your sins are forgiven and you're counted righteous, even though you still sin sometimes.

First, find **Romans 3:23–24** in your Bible and read about this present.

Write what the present is again here:

_____

Now think about why this present is awesome. Here's what some students might say:

"Great gift! I don't feel guilty or condemned anymore. I know I'm saved!"

"I don't feel like God hates me because of my sin anymore. Now I feel close to him, even when I fail sometimes."

"Wow! Being good doesn't make me feel like showing off anymore. I'm humble because my goodness comes from Jesus."

"Saved only because of Jesus! That means I can stop comparing myself with others or trying to show how much better I am. What a relief!"

Circle the response that feels like the BEST REASON why you personally love this present. Share your answer and explain why you picked it.

GOD'S PRESENT FOR YOU:
BECOMING GOD'S CHILD

Joined to Jesus, you become God's child, whom he loves, forever. He becomes your Father.

Read about this present in **1 John 3:1**.

Write what the present is again here:

_____

What are some things that make this present wonderful?
Read what the students say:

"I can ask my Father for help with any problem anything! I don't need to prove myself first. I know he loves to help me."

"I can pray to my Father anytime I want and share what's on my heart! He's always glad to listen."

"Let's see . . . if I'm God's child, and he only does what's good for me, and he controls everything . . . then everything that happens will work out for my good. Wow!"

"My Father will always keep me near, even after I die. I'll be with him forever. I'm full of hope!"

Put a smiley face next to the response that feels like the BEST REASON why you personally love this present. Share and explain your answer.

GOD'S PRESENT FOR YOU: HOLINESS

Joined to Jesus, you become a new, holy person. Now, with God helping you, you're able to work at becoming more holy and obedient to God all the time.

Romans 6:11 tells about this present. Read it now.

Write what the present is again here:

_____

What makes this such an excellent gift? Check out what the students say:

"I'm alive! I can grow as a Christian. I can stop doing disgusting, sinful things. More and more, I'm learning to do good things."

"I have a whole new heart! I'm a changed person. Now I can love what God loves."

"Now the Bible speaks to my heart. I'm working to become like Jesus— imagine that!"

"I can do things that please God! There's no pressure to make him like me, but still I get to enjoy knowing that he's happy with me when I do good things. What a thrill to honor him that way!"

"Even though I still might sin a lot, sin *doesn't* control me anymore. I can fight sin in my life—and WIN!"

Put a big heart-for-God by the response that feels like the BEST REASON why you personally love this present. Share and explain your answer.

TALK ABOUT IT

Sometimes when students are asked what it means to be saved, all they can say is that it means they're going to heaven. But the three presents you just learned about are ways your salvation starts *now*—before you ever get to heaven! List the three presents and think of several *specific examples* of ways your life is changed today when you know you have these presents from God.
Example: You might tell of something you'll no longer be scared of because you know you're God's child and he always takes good care of you.

PART 2: THE WHOLE ARMOR OF GOD

In this part of the lesson you'll learn how all those presents from God help you fight sin in your life. Using them is like putting on armor from God. The presents make you strong and confident to fight the devil, who tempts you to sin.

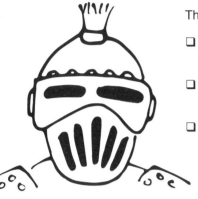

The Bible includes a letter Paul wrote to people living in the city of Ephesus.

❑ First, Paul reminded them of all God gave them because they were joined to Jesus.

❑ Then he told them to live for God. He included things that are hard to do, like telling kids to obey their parents.

❑ Then he told them how to fight when the devil tempted them to not obey—by TRUSTING GOD! He called it putting on God's armor: "Be strong in the Lord and in the strength of his might. Put on the whole armor of God, that you may be able to stand against the schemes of the devil" (Ephesians 6:10–11).

 Point to remember: When you fight to not sin, don't try to do it all by yourself. Do it by trusting God.

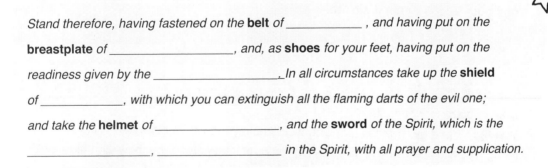

YOU WOULDN'T WANT TO FIGHT WITHOUT ARMOR, WOULD YOU? SO DON'T TRY TO FIGHT SIN WITHOUT TRUSTING GOD.

Read what Paul wrote in his letter in **Ephesians 6:14–18**. Fill in the blanks below.

*Stand therefore, having fastened on the **belt** of _____ , and having put on the*

***breastplate** of _____, and, as **shoes** for your feet, having put on the*

*readiness given by the _____.In all circumstances take up the **shield***

of _____, with which you can extinguish all the flaming darts of the evil one;

*and take the **helmet** of _____, and the **sword** of the Spirit, which is the*

_____, _____ in the Spirit, with all prayer and supplication.

Circle the last two items Paul wrote about: the Word of God and praying.

Word of God: God's message for his people. The Bible is the surest Word of God for us—always perfectly true—though God also may speak in other ways, like through preaching that's based on the Bible.

The Word of God and prayer seem different from the other pieces of God's armor, don't they? They're special pieces of armor that a believer should always be using, again and again—every day. Through them, the Holy Spirit gives us power *from God* to fight sin.

We read or listen to the Word of God (again and again, all the time).

We pray (again and again, all the time).

Here are some schemes the devil might use against you, along with ways you might fight back by trusting God and using his armor. How many pieces of armor can you match with each example? Write down each one you notice. (HINT: Each example uses prayer and/or the Word of God, plus at least one more piece of armor. Some may be used more than once.)

Truth	Righteousness	Gospel of peace Faith
Salvation	Word of God	Prayer

The devil: Tries to convince you that God hasn't done much for you, making you tired of serving God.

You fight back by: Listening to preachers and teachers who tell you the good news of how you have peace with God because Jesus has saved you—and believing that it's true!

And you do it! You serve God.

The armor you used was:

_____

The devil: Tempts you to lie to your parents.
You fight back by: Praying that God would give you strength to act like the holy, righteous person you are in Jesus.
And you do it! You tell the truth.

The armor you used was:

_____

The devil: Tells you it's okay to always try to be first in line or to get the best piece of cake or pizza for yourself.
You fight back by: Praying that God would help you think of others first (like Jesus thought of you first when he saved you), then reading in the Bible how God blesses those who are unselfish—and believing that it's true!
And you do it! You let others go first.

The armor you used was:

_____

TALK ABOUT IT

Is this the way you usually try to fight sin? Do you trust God and believe in his great presents for you, or do you just try harder by yourself to stop sinning?

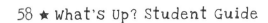

LET'S END BY ACTUALLY USING GOD'S ARMOR.

First, use the <u>Word of God</u> and remind yourself of his <u>salvation</u> by reading this Bible passage aloud together.

Praise the LORD, O my soul,
   and forget not all his benefits—

who forgives all your sins
   and heals all your diseases,

who redeems your life from the pit
   and crowns you with love and compassion,

who satisfies your desires with good things
   so that your youth is renewed like the eagle's.

From everlasting to everlasting
   the LORD's love is with those who fear him.

(Psalm 103:2–5, 17 NIV)

Now that you've been reminded how good life with God is, use <u>prayer</u>.

Write a synonym for the word "benefit." _____

<u>Underline</u> God's benefits in the passage from Psalm 103.

Pick two benefits mentioned in the passage you read. Pray as a group, each person thanking God for the gifts they picked.

Pray together that God would keep you thankful and help you resist sin.
Don't be scared to mention specific temptations you have and ask God to give you power over them.

MAKE IT STICK:

INTERVIEW AN OLDER BELIEVER

INSTRUCTIONS:

☐ Fill out this Make It Stick page during the week.

☐ Don't forget to bring your *Student Guide* back next time you meet.

☐ If you have time, go ahead and get started now.

Before the next time meeting, conduct a short interview with an older Christian to learn how they grow and obey God better. You can pick a parent or some other adult, but it should be a person who has many years of experience in following Jesus and clearly works to obey him. (HINT: If you can't think of an older believer to interview, ask your leader to be interviewed or to give you suggestions.)

Here are some ideas for questions you might ask that person. You don't have to ask all the questions, just some.

INTERVIEW QUESTIONS:

1. What's the most important thing you do that helps you grow and obey God better?

2. What's a Bible passage that's helped you grow closer to God? Why?

3. How do you pray? What have you learned about how to pray better?

4. What have you given up for Jesus?

Listen carefully to the older Christian and learn from that person. Write down what you find out on the notes page and be ready to report back what you learned the next time you meet.

OLDER BELIEVER INTERVIEW NOTES

What's the most important thing you do that helps you grow and obey God better?

What's a Bible passage that's helped you grow closer to God? Why?

How do you pray? What have you learned about how to pray better?

What have you given up for Jesus?

Other questions you want to ask:

LESSON 6

BUT I'M A GOOD PERSON

Big Idea: Two Kinds of Repentance

BEFORE YOU BEGIN

Report on your interview with the older believer. What did you learn about the Christian life? Did anything surprise you?

Did the older believer tell you something about **fighting sin**? If so, share it with the group.

Did the older believer tell you something about **trusting Jesus**? If so, share it with the group.

TODAY'S LESSON

Think about how you breathe. You INHALE and you EXHALE. They go together. You can't do one without the other. You can't live unless you do *both*.

The Christian life is like breathing. You fight sin (we call that REPENTANCE) and you trust Jesus (we call that FAITH). They always go together. You need *both* in order to live and grow as a Christian. That's what you'll learn about today.

PART 1: TWO KINDS OF REPENTANCE

In this section, you'll learn how you can also think of REPENTANCE and FAITH as two difference kinds of repentance.

Jesus talked about both when he first started preaching. Read what he said:

> *"The kingdom of God is at hand; repent and believe in the gospel."* (Mark 1:15)

Underline the two things Jesus said to do.

Belief in the gospel means the same thing as faith. Let's define the two things Jesus said to do.

Repent: Stop living a wrong way and start living a new, godly way.

Have faith: Believe that Jesus died for your sin and trust him—not your own good behavior to make you right with God.

Point to remember:
To become a Christian, *start* practicing repentance and faith in Jesus.
To grow as a Christian, *keep* practicing repentance and faith in Jesus.

"I thought only bad people needed to repent."

"So did I. But it looks like everyone has to repent, and God's people keep at it all their lives."

Did you see how FAITH includes stopping a wrong way to live? You have to stop trusting your own good behavior. So faith includes a kind of repentance too. Faith means you repent of your self-justification.

REPENTANCE TYPE #1:
REPENT OF YOUR *BAD* BEHAVIOR.

Stop living a life of sin.

Start obeying God instead.

REPENTANCE TYPE #2:
REPENT OF YOUR *SELF-JUSTIFICATION.*

Stop trying to prove to God that you're righteous.

Start believing instead that God counts you righteous because you have faith in Jesus.

Draw a (circle) around the type of repentance that seems harder to you. Are you mostly . . .

A SINNER

You try to make yourself happy by being BAD and living however you want.

You especially need to repent of your BAD BEHAVIOR.

OR

A SELF-JUSTIFIER

You try to earn a happy life by being GOOD and living how you're supposed to (and you compare yourself to others and get jealous).

You especially need to repent of your SELF-JUSTIFICATION.

TALK ABOUT IT

Tell why that kind of repentance is harder for you.

PART 2: THE TWO SONS

For the rest of this lesson, you'll study a story Jesus told about two sons. Each son especially needed one type of repentance.

First read about the crowd that heard Jesus's story. They needed to repent too.

> *Now the tax collectors and sinners were all drawing near to hear him. And the Pharisees and the scribes grumbled, saying, "This man receives sinners and eats with them."* *(Luke 15:1–2)*

Jesus told his story to two kinds of people. Which groups do you think were people who did BAD things and needed to repent of their <u>bad behavior</u>?

_____ and _____

Which groups do you think were people who did GOOD things, but compared themselves to others and needed to repent of their <u>self-justification</u>?

_____ and _____

Tax collectors in those days cheated people to get rich (obviously BAD!). Pharisees were a group of people who worked hard to obey God (obviously GOOD!). But Jesus wanted both kinds of people to see that they need him.

Did you notice how the younger son asked for his inheritance while the father was still alive? That's like saying you wish your father were dead already! Then he went out and wasted it.

Character sketch:
Younger Son

Now do a character sketch of the younger son in this first part of the story. Think of at least four adjectives that describe his character. Write them next to his picture. If you need help thinking of words to describe him, consider these questions:

❑ What is his attitude?

❑ How does he feel about others?

❑ How well does he contribute to his family?

❑ What is it about him that gets him into trouble?

Also consider what the younger son thinks will make him happy in life. Write a sentence in the thought bubble that describes what he's hoping for at the start of the story.

Share and discuss the words and sentences you thought of.

Finally, circle the description that best fits the younger son.

A SINNER

You try to make yourself happy by being BAD and living however you want.

You especially need to repent of your BAD BEHAVIOR.

OR

A SELF-JUSTIFIER

You try to earn a happy life by being GOOD and living how you're supposed to (and you compare yourself to others and get jealous).

You especially need to repent of your SELF-JUSTIFICATION.

Now read what happened with the younger son in verses 17–24.

The younger son repented! He went home and found the father to be more loving than he ever imagined. Only a father—the best father you could imagine—could have *that* much love. It was humiliating for an older man in Jesus's day to run. But the father was so happy to see his son that he ran to greet him!

List six other things the father did because he was so happy to see his son.

1. _____

2. _____

3. _____

4. _____

5. _____

6. _____

The father in the story is like God. What do you think Jesus wanted the sinners who were listening to his story to know about God? Write your answer in a sentence below or discuss with the group.

_____

_____

_____

_____

The story isn't over. Read verses 25–32 to learn what the older son did when he heard about the celebration.

Character Sketch: Older Son

Now do a character sketch of the older son. Again think of adjectives that describe him, and write them next to his picture.
If you need help, consider these questions:

❏ How well does he contribute to his family and work for his father?

❏ How might he compare himself to his younger brother?

❏ How does he feel about the party?

❏ What is his attitude toward his father?

Then imagine what the older son thinks is the way to be happy and get good things in life. Write a sentence in the thought bubble that describes his plan to get approval from the father and feel good about himself.

Share and discuss the words and sentences you thought of.

Now circle the description that best fits the older son.

A SINNER

You try to make yourself happy by being BAD and living however you want.

You especially need to repent of your BAD BEHAVIOR.

OR

A SELF-JUSTIFIER

You try to earn a happy life by being GOOD and living how you're supposed to (and you compare yourself to others and get jealous).

You especially need to repent of your SELF-JUSTIFICATION.

Character Sketch: Father

There's one more character sketch to do. It's for the most important character in the story—the father. Refer back to the story in your Bible if necessary. Write some adjectives that describe him next to his picture.

Also fill in two thought bubbles for the father:

❑ **First thought bubble:** Imagine what the father is thinking now that his younger son has repented of his sin.

❑ **Second thought bubble:** Imagine what the father hopes for his older son.

Share and discuss what you wrote.

TALK ABOUT IT

Jesus's story about the two sons matters when YOU need to repent.

SITUATION #1: You've <u>behaved </u>badly by living your way instead of God's way.

What should you remember about your Father in heaven? How does he feel about his children who've behaved badly?

SITUATION #2: You're trying <u>self-justification</u>, hoping to earn God's love by being good.

Now what should you remember about your Father in heaven? How does he feel about his children who've tried to justify themselves?

The father in Jesus's story told the older son, "Everything I have is yours." Wow! Here's a list of some of the things you already have from God and don't need to earn if you have faith in Jesus.

- ❑ God loves you perfectly, forever. (Psalm 136:1)

- ❑ God adopts you as his own son/daughter. (John 1:12)

- ❑ God promises to never leave you for any reason. (Hebrews 13:5)

- ❑ God makes everything work for your good. (Romans 8:28)

- ❑ God gives you an inheritance in heaven that you can't lose. (1 Peter 1:4)

- ❑ God will give you eternal joy with him. (Revelation 7:17)

PRAY ABOUT IT

Make your closing prayer today a prayer of thanksgiving for the items on that list. Thank God for many of them, checking them off as you mention them to him. Then pray that he will help you believe that he's *that* good and loving. Pray that this will help you repent of both your <u>bad behavior</u> and your <u>self-justification</u>.

MAKE IT STICK:

SPEND TIME WITH YOUR FATHER

INSTRUCTIONS:

❑ Fill out this Make It Stick page during the week.

❑ Don't forget to bring your *Student Guide* back next time you meet.

Jesus's story about the two sons was actually the last in a series of three similar parables. In each one, something is lost and the person who lost it has a great celebration when it's found.

Your task until the next session is to spend time with your Father in prayer *every day*, thanking him for the love and compassion he had for you when you were still lost in sin. He celebrates how you're saved! So this week, celebrate with him.

Do three things in each day's time with God (yes, the same thing each day):

1. Read the first two stories in Luke 15:1–10.

2. Remember how lost you were before God saved you. You were *dead* in sin.

3. Thank God in your own words for the amazing love he has for someone like you: "But God, being rich in mercy, because of the great love with which he loved us, even when we were dead in our trespasses, made us alive together with Christ—by grace you have been saved" (Ephesians 2:4–5).

Each day, after you pray, write down one thing you thanked God for in your prayer.

Day One:
Thank you, Father, that you _____ me.

Day Two:
Thank you, Father, that you _____ me.

Day Three:
Thank you, Father, that you _____ me.

Day Four:
Thank you, Father, that you _____ me.

Day Five:
Thank you, Father, that you _____ me.

Day Six
Thank you, Father, that you _____ me.

Day Seven:
Thank you, Father, that you _____ me.

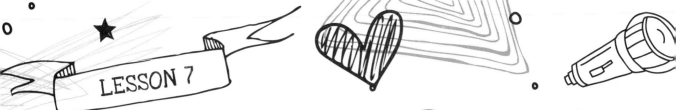

DO I LOVE GOD? UM...

Big Idea: Big Forgiveness and Big Love

BEFORE YOU BEGIN

Tell about the time you spent with your Father reading Luke 15 and praying.
Tell what things you liked about it or what you didn't like about it.

Did you get **bored**? _____ Yes _____ No

If you're bored with God, it might mean you trust other things besides Jesus to really make you happy.

<u>So next time you pray</u>: Repent of your sin (how you love other things more than Jesus). Confess your sin to your Father and ask him to help you see the beauty of Jesus.

Did it make you **uncomfortable**? _____ Yes _____ No

If you aren't comfortable with God, it might mean you feel your behavior isn't good enough for him. Remember that you may always pray to God—not because you're good enough, but because you're joined to Jesus and have his righteousness.

<u>So next time you pray</u>: Repent of your self-justification. Your Father loves for you to come to him no matter how bad you've been.

Wouldn't it be nice to love God so much that you're always eager to spend time with your Father? Today you'll learn how your love for Jesus can grow—when you admit you're a sinner!

PART 1: TWO CHOICES WHEN YOU SIN

Let's start by learning about two choices you have when you realize you've sinned. Read this story:

When I was a new Christian, I began to read my Bible as often as I could. One day as I was reading how God hated sin, and how our sin separates us from him, I thought, *Since God hates sin so much, today I won't sin the entire day. I am going to have a sin-free day!*

As soon as I finished thinking I could have a "sin-free" day, I saw my brother riding my bike without my permission. The next instant I was outside and yelling at him to get off my bike. How dare he touch my stuff!

Then it hit me. Oh, no! I was being selfish. I couldn't keep sin out of my life for even five seconds, let alone a whole day. For the first time, I saw how big my sin was!

Yikes! I was in big trouble!

Maybe you've had an experience like that. You realized how terribly hard it is to not sin for even a short while. When you realize what a big sinner you are, you have **two choices**.

CHOICE #1:

You can <u>try to ignore your sin or hide it</u>, like these students.

Why will it be hard for those students to grow as Christians when they're thinking these ways? Discuss.

CHOICE #2:

The other choice is to <u>admit you're a horrible sinner</u>. That's what we'll do in the next several lessons. To complete these lessons, you're going to have to think and talk LOTS about your own sin and the ways you do wrong. It'll be SIN, SIN, SIN.

How does that sound to you? Check all the lines that apply.

___ It sounds like **no fun**. I might end up feeling bad about myself. I wish we could pretend God doesn't care so much about sin.

___ It sounds like it might be **embarrassing**. I need to think of some not-so-bad sins I can tell about—so I can avoid telling about my very worst ones.

___ It sounds **scary**. I don't like thinking about myself that way, or what might happen to me because of my sin.

TALK ABOUT IT

Show the group which lines you checked. If none of them are what you feel when you have to talk about your sin, tell what you do feel.

Whenever you try to ignore or hide your sin, it's <u>hard for you to grow</u>.

❑ Because you're **scared** or **unhappy** when you hear how God feels about sin, you won't enjoy studying about him or reading the Bible. You'll stop learning about God.

❑ Because you're too **scared** or **embarrassed** to admit your sin, you'll keep hiding it. Instead of learning new ways to repent, you'll pretend you don't have to repent.

PART 2: SIMON AND THE SINFUL WOMAN

Now let's study a Bible story from **Luke 7:36–47**. First learn about the characters and the occasion.

Simon
(a Pharisee)

Respected in the city

Well-known as a person who worked hard to obey God

Everyone thought, "Good for you!"

Sinful Woman

Had a bad reputation in the city

Well-known as a person who did sinful things

Everyone thought, "Shame on you!"

OCCASION:

A meal, hosted by Simon, which Jesus attended

Anyone in the city could watch and listen, but only invited guests could sit and eat

Very honored guests were greeted by Simon with a kiss

Guests with master status had their feet washed by a servant

THE STORY BEGINS:
A dinner surprise

Read through verse 39 and answer the questions below.

Which character focuses on the sins of others instead of his/her own sins?

_____

Which character thinks him/herself so good he/she can judge others?

_____

Is this "good" person the same character who most shows love to Jesus?

_____

THE STORY CONTINUES:
Jesus explains

Read vv. 40–47.

Jesus said having sins forgiven is like owing money and having the debt canceled so you don't have to pay.

Circle the one that makes you most thankful.

Not having to pay 500 coins

?

Not having to pay 50 coins

Circle the character who loved Jesus most.

Woman who was forgiven for MUCH sin

Simon who was forgiven little

Do you think Simon really didn't sin much? Or do you think his sin was just less obvious or better hidden? Discuss why you think so.

For each statement, write whether you suspect it better fits Simon or the woman.

_____ Was so sorry for sin it made him/her cry.

_____ Knew his/her life had been shameful.

_____ Thought his/her life was a model for others.

_____ Had little joy over being forgiven and seldom thought about it much.

_____ Was uninterested in loving Jesus.

_____ Was eager to show love for Jesus.

TALK ABOUT IT

Now look back over the list. Which statements best describe <u>you</u>? Share how you're like Simon or like the sinful woman.

The woman knew how big and shameful her sin was. Remember, everyone thought "shame on you!" about her.

When Jesus forgives your sin, he takes away your guilt and shame. When he died on the cross, people passing by thought he was a criminal. They thought "shame on you!"—about HIM! That's what <u>you</u> deserve, but Jesus took it in your place.

The MORE you understand how shameful your sin is and how he took <u>all</u> of that **guilt** and **punishment** and **shame** for you on the cross, the MORE you will love him! *That's* how you grow.

PART 3: THE CROSS FIGURE

The four parts of the cross figure will help you understand how important it is to admit that your sin is BIG and to believe that your forgiveness in Jesus is BIG too.

Cross figure part 1 shows your life when you're a new Christian. The light stands for two things you see when you believe. First, you see how holy God is and how he wants you to be holy too (the top of the beam of light). Second, you see how sinful and unholy you actually are (the bottom of the beam of light).

PICTURE 1: I AM A NEW CHRISTIAN

I see God's _____

I see my _____

"That's good. I'm happy and thankful for Jesus."

"There's a lot of space between what God demands from me and the sin I actually do."

"Of course there is. But do you see how the cross of Jesus spans the gap between God's holy demands and your sinfulness? Because of Jesus, you're forgiven."

INSTRUCTIONS:

1. Draw yourself holding the light.

2. Write "holiness" on the line by the top beam of light.

3. Write "sinfulness" on the line by the bottom beam.

4. Fill in the cross to show how God accepts you anyway because of Jesus.

The second part of the cross figure shows that you've learned MORE about God's holy demands. You've also learned MORE about how sinful you are. The beam of light is growing wider.

PICTURE 2: I LEARN MORE

I see MORE of God's holiness.

I see MORE of my sinfulness.

Gap

Gap

The gaps make me:

_____

_____

_____

"I can see I'm a much bigger sinner than I first thought. But look, the cross has stayed the same size as it was before. Oh, no! This makes me nervous."

"I feel like I'm not good enough for God. I need to fix this!"

"Your problem is you didn't also learn more about how completely Jesus forgives you. You didn't believe and trust him even more than before. Now there are gaps."

INSTRUCTIONS:

1. Fill in the too-small cross that won't let you feel completely accepted by God.

2. Write the words "scared," "unhappy," and "embarrassed" on the blank lines.

In the third part of the cross figure, you start pretending. Because you're worried and embarrassed at not being good enough, you try to fill in the gaps yourself. You pretend God really doesn't care so much about some sins. Or you make excuses for your sin so you'll look like a better person than you really are.

PICTURE 3: I FAKE IT

I see MORE of God's holiness.

I see MORE of my sinfulness.

"You still think I'm a good person, don't you? Oh, I hope so! I think God is happy enough if I'm basically good. And I don't do any big sins. None at all. Really."

"Hmmm. It sounds like you're just trying to look good so people will think well of you."

"Okay, you're right. Actually, I'm faking my Christian life. I don't like learning about God, and I hide my sin or make excuses for it. Inside, I'm nervous about not being good enough."

INSTRUCTIONS:

1. In the top box write, "I pretend God doesn't mind my sin."

2. In the bottom box write, "I pretend I'm better than I really am."

In part 4 of the cross figure, you stop pretending and start trusting Jesus MORE instead. You admit your sin is huge, but you believe that God still forgives all of it because Jesus died for you. The cross and all that Jesus does for you seems *that big* to you because you're trusting him *that much!*

PICTURE 4: I CAN REALLY GROW

I see MORE of God's holiness.

I see MORE of my sinfulness.

What Jesus does for me seems bigger too! I believe MORE that I am:

_____

_____

_____

_____

_____

because of Jesus.

"I've learned that my sin is so big I have no chance of covering it up with excuses. But good news! God loves me SO much that he still forgives me for all that yucky sin."

"It feels good to have bigger belief, doesn't it?"

"Yes. Now that I believe in Jesus MORE, all that he does for me seems bigger. Instead of trusting my excuses to make me look good, I trust Jesus to forgive everything. Now I can learn about God and admit my sin and enjoy it! I can grow! I love Jesus more too."

INSTRUCTIONS:

1. Fill in the larger cross that covers all your sin.

2. On the lines write:

    *   "forgiven"

    *   "loved"

    *   "accepted"

    *   "righteous"

    *   "unashamed"

Part 4 of the cross figure teaches that whenever you sin you have **two choices.**

Choice 1 → When I Sin → Get scared. Make excuses. Try to make myself look better than I am. → No growth. No love for Jesus.

Choice 2 → When I Sin → Admit it. Trust Jesus. Believe that he died for all my sin. His love for me is that big! → Growth. Bigger love for Jesus.

Which choice treats Jesus's death as a little thing you don't need very much?
Which treats it as a big thing that means the world to you?

TALK ABOUT IT

How would your behavior change if you made the second choice more often?

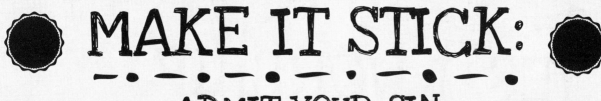

MAKE IT STICK:
ADMIT YOUR SIN

INSTRUCTIONS:

❑ Fill out this Make It Stick page during the week.

❑ Don't forget to bring your *Student Guide* back next time you meet.

❑ If you have time, go ahead and get started now.

Memorize 1 John 1:8–9.

If we say we have no sin, we deceive ourselves, and the truth is not in us. If we confess our sins, he is faithful and just to forgive us our sins and to cleanse us from all unrighteousness.

Fill your name in the first part of the verse:

If I, _____, say that I have no sin, I, _____, deceive myself and the truth is not in me.

This week, notice when you: try to defend yourself or make excuses for your sin, instead of stopping, admitting you were wrong, and asking forgiveness.

Below, write a few sentences about . . .

. . . a time this week when you caught yourself making excuses for your sin, and how the situation could have been different if you'd admitted your sin and asked forgiveness instead, or

. . . a time this week when you remembered to admit your sin instead of hiding it, and how it felt to do this.

_____

_____

_____

_____

_____

_____

_____

_____

_____

LESSON 8

YES, I WORSHIP IDOLS

Big Idea: Real-Life Idols

BEFORE YOU BEGIN

Share what you wrote about a time when you caught yourself making excuses for your sin. Did you remember to admit your sin and seek forgiveness instead?

Why do you think that's often hard to do?

TODAY'S LESSON

It may have been hard for you this week to admit your sin, ask God to forgive you, and repent. One reason is that we secretly like our sin. Our sin <u>feels good</u> to us while we're doing it. This is because there are things in our lives that we love, trust, or fear more than God. The Bible calls these things IDOLS.

Does the idea of worshiping idols sound silly to you? Well, people who worship idols made of wood and stone have their reasons—some of them not so silly! And *you* have reasons why you're tempted to worship your own kind of idols, too.

Yes, this lesson is about *your* idols.

❑ First, you'll learn why people in Bible times worshiped *their* idols.

❑ Second, you'll find out what some of *your* idols are.

❑ Third, you'll see why Jesus is better than any idols—even yours.

PART 1: WHY WOULD ANYONE WORSHIP AN IDOL?

Let's learn about idols in Bible times. Read what some idol worshipers have to say, and answer the questions.

Idol: BAAL   **Date:** 870 BC   **Place:** SIDON, PHOENECIA

"I worship Baal because I'm a farmer and we need rain to grow food and survive. Baal wakes up every fall and sends thunderstorms. He throws lightning bolts and makes it pour rain!

It's important that I worship Baal by giving him sacrifices. I also help wake him up every year by joining wild parties at his temple. The parties give him energy to wake up and send rain. The priests at the temple cut themselves with swords too. All their gushing blood helps get Baal's attention.

I need to please Baal because without his rain we'd die. Plus, I enjoy the wild parties. They're naughty fun!"

What does the worshiper <u>love</u> about Baal?

_____

How does he <u>trust</u> Baal to care for him?

_____

What does he <u>fear</u> that makes him worship Baal?

_____

Idol: ATHENA   Date: 49 AD   Place: Athens, Greece

"We Greeks worship many gods. They all have temples here in Athens. My favorite goddess, Athena, stands for wisdom, happy home life, and solid families.

I take great pride in my city. Our devotion to Athena and wisdom makes us the smartest people in the world. Philosophers everywhere look up to us. I serve Athena by studying wisdom. I also bring gifts to her temple, the Parthenon. Worshiping her keeps my family life happy.

I keep this up because I wouldn't want her to feel neglected. She can get grumpy, you know. If I don't worship her, she might do something mean to disrupt my happy home life."

What does the worshiper <u>love</u> about Athena?

_____

How does she <u>trust</u> Athena to care for her?

_____

What does she <u>fear</u> that makes her worship Athena?

_____

TALK ABOUT IT

Now discuss what you learned about idol worship. Even though Baal worshipers and Athena worshipers want very different things, how are the worship of Baal and Athena similar?

HAVING IDOLS IS ABOUT:

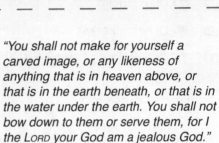

1. What you <u>love (instead of God)</u>

2. What you <u>trust (instead of God)</u>

3. What you <u>fear (instead of believing God will protect you)</u>

Now learn what God thinks of idols and worship. Draw a line from each statement below to a phrase in the Bible that tells about it.

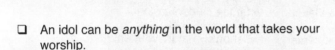

❑ An idol can be *anything* in the world that takes your worship.

❑ An idol is something you make for yourself to control your own life—instead of letting God be in control.

❑ Anything you're greedy for and want more than you want God is an idol.

❑ God HATES idols. He's jealous for your worship.

*"You shall not make for yourself a carved image, or any likeness of anything that is in heaven above, or that is in the earth beneath, or that is in the water under the earth. You shall not bow down to them or serve them, for I the L*ORD *your God am a jealous God."* (Exodus 20:4–5)

Put to death, therefore . . . greed, which is idolatry. (Colossians 3:5 NIV)

PART 2: WHAT IDOLS MIGHT *YOU* WORSHIP?

You probably don't worship Baal or Athena, but anything you <u>love</u> more than God, <u>trust</u> more than God, or <u>fear losing</u> more than God is *an idol to you*.

> **Point to remember:**
> An idol is *anything* that takes God's place in your life.

Here are some examples.

☐ ♥ Draw a **heart** next to the sentence that shows what the student <u>loves</u>.

☐ ★ Draw a **star** next to the sentence that shows what the student <u>trusts</u>.

☐ 💧 Draw a **drop of sweat** next to the sentence that shows what the student <u>fears</u>.

Idol: MONEY

"I dream about being able to buy anything I want."

"I feel safe because I know my parents have plenty of money."

"Being poor would be the worst!"

Idol:
APPROVAL OF FRIENDS

Spend a few minutes thinking about what your own idols might be. To identify your idols, consider what you daydream about, or what makes you angry if you don't get it. Now check those things in this list that are idols in YOUR life. What do you love, trust, or fear not having more than God?

_____ Being first or important

_____ Being popular with friends

_____ Success in school

_____ Success in sports

_____ Success in _____

_____ Approval of parents

_____ Approval of teachers

_____ Approval of _____

_____ Money

_____ Movies or TV

_____ Video games or toys

_____ Family

_____ Being noticed or famous

_____ Good looks (or not looking dorky)

_____ Never being laughed at

_____ Being thought of as smart

_____ Long life and health

_____ Acceptance by others

_____ Being included in fun things

_____ Getting my fair share

_____ Being talented

_____ Good reputation

_____ Comfortable life

_____ Recognition for what I'm good at

TALK ABOUT IT

Some things in the list are good things, aren't they? But if you love, trust, or fear not having them more than you do God, they're still dangerous idols—even more dangerous because they look like good things!

Share with the group what some of your most dangerous idols are. Tell what you do that shows they're idols in your life.

Now choose one idol from those you checked on the last page. Pick one that's especially tempting to you. Draw a picture of it as if it were a Bible-times statue kind of idol. Also draw a picture of yourself, the idol worshiper, explaining how you serve that idol.

Example: *If your idol is being smart or looking smart to others, you might draw a statue holding textbooks and wearing nerdy glasses. Then you might write one of the following:*

❑ I love <u>looking smart</u>, so I <u>show off how much I know</u>.

❑ I trust <u>being smart</u>, so I <u>study hard because it'll make me successful</u>.

❑ I fear <u>people thinking I'm stupid</u>, so I <u>can't stand when they think I don't know something</u>.

PART 3: WHAT'S BETTER THAN IDOLS?

Serving idols is like drinking seawater. If you were adrift in a lifeboat with nothing but seawater around you, drinking it would feel good at first. But soon that salty water would kill you.

It's the same with your idols. It feels good to serve them. Often it feels like you just *have* to serve them. But they're deadly. They can't really satisfy you.

❑ ONLY the living God is worth your love.

❑ ONLY the living God is always trustworthy.

❑ ONLY the living God can conquer what you fear.

❑ ONLY Jesus is the living water—fresh water that quenches your thirst.

The apostle Paul preached in Athens once. He spoke right next to the temple where people worshiped the idol Athena. Read what he said about the true God.

The God who made the world and everything in it, being Lord of heaven and earth, does not live in temples made by man, nor is he served by human hands, as though he needed anything, since he himself gives to all mankind life and breath and everything. (Acts 17:24–25)

<u>Underline</u> at least three things that make the true God better than Athena.

Put a star next to the one thing that you're most thankful is true about God.

God sent someone to speak to Baal worshipers too. The prophet Elijah had a contest with the priests of Baal to see whether Baal or the true God could send lightning and rain. Nothing happened when Baal's priests yelled and cut themselves and made their blood flow. But when Elijah prayed to the true God, he sent fire from heaven.

Read what Elijah said in his prayer.

> *O LORD, answer me, so these people may know that you, O LORD, are God, and that you are turning their hearts back again. (1 Kings 18:37 NIV)*

Underline the two things Elijah prayed for the people to know about God.

What does God do for the hearts of his people?

_____

Your idolatry is very bad, but you can turn back to Jesus. He's not at all like idols!

❑   Idols have no real power, but Jesus does.

❑   Idols promise that you can earn happiness by being devoted to them, but Jesus saves us for free.

❑   Idols are harsh. Baal's priests cut themselves trying to serve him. But Jesus bled for us! Serving him is joyful thanksgiving, not harsh duty.

End by praying to the true God. Your prayer should have two parts:

1.   **Thanks.** Even though you struggle with many idols, be thankful that Jesus died for you—an idol worshiper! Thank him that Jesus bled for you. Also praise him for whatever you put a star next to in Paul's sermon at Athens.

2.   **Request.** Ask God to turn your heart away from the idols in your life and back to him. Look back at the things you checked as idols in your life. Pray about each one, asking God to turn your heart away from it.

MAKE IT STICK:
NOTICE YOUR IDOL WORSHIP

INSTRUCTIONS:

- ❏ Fill out this Make It Stick page during the week.
- ❏ Don't forget to bring your *Student Guide* back next time you meet.
- ❏ If you have time, go ahead and get started now.

It's important to notice idols in your life so you can repent of them and act more like the holy person God has made you. On the line below, write one idol that's especially tempting to you. (If you like, also draw a picture of what an actual stone or wooden idol of what you worship might look like.)

At the end of each day in the coming week, think of something specific you did that day because of the idol you mentioned above. Write the specific thing you did on the line below.

DAY ONE
What I did today because of my idol: _____

DAY TWO
What I did today because of my idol: _____

DAY THREE
What I did today because of my idol: _____

DAY FOUR
What I did today because of my idol: _____

DAY FIVE
What I did today because of my idol: _____

DAY SIX
What I did today because of my idol: _____

DAY SEVEN
What I did today because of my idol: _____

Because idol worship is sin, pray to God when you write down your behavior.

Ask him to forgive your sin.

Thank him that you may turn back to him again and again—every time you catch yourself worshiping an idol—and *always* be forgiven!

Ask him to turn your heart away from that idol and toward him.

Praise him for how he's better than that idol.

LOOK! SHARK!

Big Idea: Confronting Unbelief

BEFORE YOU BEGIN

Share some of the ways you caught yourself serving an idol in your life. What did you learn about how your sin is connected to idols deep in your heart?

Do you think your sin is mostly connected to:

- Something you <u>love</u> more than you love God,

- Something you <u>trust</u> more than you trust God, or

- Something you <u>fear</u> instead of trusting God?

TODAY'S LESSON

Have you ever had someone tell you, "I have some good news and some bad news; which would you like to hear first?"? Which would you want to hear first: good news or bad?

Today's lesson starts with more bad news about your sin and idols. Sin is an even bigger, deeper problem than you may realize. You'll learn about it in three steps:

1. You'll look at two case studies of sinners in the Bible. You'll see how hidden sin, deep in their hearts, led them to sin outwardly.

2. You'll think about your own deep sins.

3. The good news! You'll see how to fight that deep sin by believing the gospel.

It's all about how sin is like a shark, lurking under the surface of your life.

PART 1: SINNERS AND THE SHARK

Case Study 1:
Abram

Sins:

- **Lying**

- **Telling his wife to lie**

- **Giving up his wife while he got rich**

Abram was a man with much faith in God, but even he had idols. His story comes near the beginning of the Bible, and starts with God giving him great promises. Underline at least six things God told Abram he would do for him.

"I will make of you a great nation, and I will bless you and make your name great, so that you will be a blessing. I will bless those who bless you, and him who dishonors you I will curse, and in you all the families of the earth shall be blessed." (Genesis 12:2–3)

Now read **Genesis 12:10–19** to see what Abram did shortly after that, then answer the questions below.

Abram told a huge lie and got lots of people in trouble! He sinned because there was an idol of fear in his life. What was he afraid of that led him to lie?

_____

TALK ABOUT IT

What if Abram had more fully believed the promises God had told him earlier? Discuss how his trip to Egypt might have been different.

Think of sin as a shark. If you were swimming in the ocean and saw a large fin sticking out of the water, would you just ignore it? No! You'd know there was something more dangerous lurking under the surface—a shark! Our sin is like that. The sins we can see tell us there's something even more dangerous under the surface, inside our hearts, that's making us sin.

Let's see how that worked with Abram. On the line above the water, near the shark fin, write "lying." That's how Abram sinned in Egypt.

Sin you can see:

_____

The idol under the sin:
Abram had love / trust / fear of:

_____

The deepest sin of all—UNBELIEF:
Abram didn't really believe God, that:

_____

Under the water, near the shark, circle how Abram's idol that caused him to do the sins we could see was a "fear" idol. He was scared he might be killed. So write "being killed" on the second line.

But the biggest, deepest sin lurking in Abram's heart was **unbelief**:

Question:
Why did Abram sin?

Answer:
He **feared** he might be killed.

Question:
But *why* did he fear?

Answer:
Because he **didn't fully believe** God would bless him and keep him alive to become a great nation like God had promised.

So on the bottom line write "he would bless him like he promised." That was Abram's unbelief.

Point to remember:
Not believing God is the big, deep, dangerous sin that leads to all the others.

Case Study 2:

Ananias and Sapphira

Sins:

- **Lying**
- **Pretending to be generous**

Ananias and Sapphira were part of the church in Jerusalem not long after Jesus lived on earth. The people in that church loved belonging to Jesus so much that they shared everything they owned with each other. One man named Barnabus even sold an expensive field and gave all the money to the apostles to help needy people in the church. That was impressive! Ananias and Sapphira decided they wanted to look impressive too. Read **Acts 5:1–10** to see what happened.

TALK ABOUT IT

Ananias and Sapphira pretended to give all the money they got to the church so they would look good, like Barnabas. Discuss what you think their idols were. Think of several things.

Now use the shark to understand Ananias and Sapphira's sin. For the sin you can see, write "lying and pretending."

Sin you can see:

The idol under the sin:

Ananias & Sapphira had love / trust / fear of:

The deepest sin of all—UNBELIEF:

Ananias & Sapphira didn't really believe God, that:

The Bible doesn't say what Ananias and Sapphira were thinking, so we have to guess what their idol was. Maybe one idol was that they trusted money and wanted to keep some in case of emergencies. Their biggest idol, though, seems to be that they loved being famous and popular and having a good reputation in the church. So circle love and then write "a good reputation in the church" on the line for their idol.

But as always, the biggest, deepest sin lurking in their hearts was **unbelief**.

Question:

Why did Ananias and Sapphira sin?

Answer:

They **loved** having a good reputation in the church.

Question:

But *why* did they love a good reputation?

Answer:

Because they **didn't fully believe** that just belonging to Jesus and serving him is far better than being famous and popular. He gives *everything* good we need.

So on the bottom line write "Jesus is better than being popular and gives us all we need."

PART 2: YOU AND THE SHARK

Read **Mark 7:21–23** to learn what Jesus said about where our sin comes from. Write the answer below.

Jesus says our sin comes

_____

Jesus agrees you have a shark under the surface—a big sin problem deep inside you. Because sin comes from your heart, just trying not to sin or staying away from bad influences won't stop your sin. You have a heart problem. When you sin, something other than Jesus has become more important to your heart. You need to believe more deeply that Jesus is better.

Look at some examples of how that might work, using the shark:

My Sin you can See:

telling lies

My idol under this sin:

I had love / trust / fear of:
(circle one)

people might think less of me if they knew the truth

I don't really believe God, that:

he thinks the world of me no matter what I'm like

What other people think of me has become more important to my heart than the good news.

My Sin you can See:

taking the biggest piece of cake or pizza

My idol under this sin:

I had love / trust / fear of:
(circle one)

always being greedy to have the most or best for myself

I don't really believe God, that:

in Jesus he gives me all I need, and so much heavenly blessing-so I can easily let others have the best worldly things

Worldly things have become more important to my heart than this good news.

Now practice with some of your own sins. Pick some outward sins you do often. Then fill in what they show about the shark in your heart.

My Sin you can See:

My idol under this sin:
I had love / trust / fear of:
(circle one)

I don't really believe God, that:

My Sin you can See:

My idol under this sin:
I had love / trust / fear of:
(circle one)

I don't really believe God, that:

TALK ABOUT IT

Discuss what you wrote. If necessary, ask others in the group to help you understand what about Jesus you fail to believe.

"This could get depressing. My sin problem goes so deep I have no chance at all of fixing it!"

"It's true that you can't fix it. But God's Spirit changes hearts! He helps us to believe."

PART 3: SHOOTING THE SHARK

You wouldn't hunt a shark by shooting at its fin. You'd aim at the shark's body under the water. In the same way, the most important part of fighting sin is to aim at your heart. You need to aim deep. Start by believing how much Jesus loves you.

READ WHAT PAUL WROTE IN THE BOOK OF EPHESIANS.

For this reason I kneel before the Father, from whom his whole family in heaven and on earth derives its name. I pray that out of his glorious riches he may strengthen you with power through his Spirit in your inner being, so that Christ may dwell in your hearts through faith. And I pray that you, being rooted and established in love, may have power, together with all the saints, to grasp how wide and long and high and deep is the love of Christ, and to know this love that surpasses knowledge. (Ephesians 3:14–19 NIV)

Where does the Spirit work to strengthen you with power?

_____

In what part of you does Christ dwell?

_____

What does God's work in you give you power to grasp (understand)?

_____

If you're joined to Jesus, you CAN fight your sin—successfully! You can *shoot that shark*, because God's Spirit is in your heart, changing you on the inside, helping you to know and believe his love more deeply.

Finish by praying, like Paul did. Pray two things:

1. Thank God for the many, many ways he loves you and cares for you. Mention some that have come up in this lesson or in other recent lessons. Make a list here of ways God is kind to you, and refer to it when you pray.

    _____

    _____

    _____

    _____

2. Ask God to help you believe that everything he says about his love for you is true. Pray that you will know "how wide and long and high and deep is the love of Christ"—and will believe it!

MAKE IT STICK:

THE SHARK CHART

INSTRUCTIONS:

- ❑ Fill out this Make It Stick page during the week.

- ❑ Don't forget to bring your *Student Guide* back next time you meet.

- ❑ If you have time, go ahead and get started now.

Use the Shark Chart to keep a record of some of the sins in your life.
As you catch yourself having sinned:

1. Write down the sin.

2. Then figure out what's the idol "under the surface."

3. Then write down what you failed to believe about Jesus.

Remember always to pray as you think about your sin. Ask God to forgive you (he surely will!) and to help your heart to believe. The Holy Spirit fights that shark right alongside you!

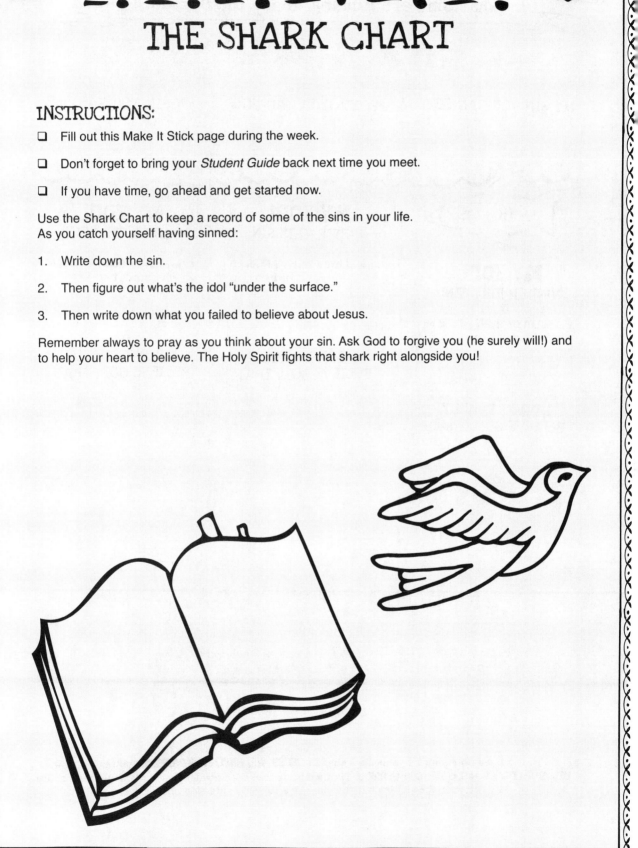

THE SHARK CHART

what sins are lurking under the surface?

MY SIN YOU CAN SEE: | MY SIN YOU CAN SEE: | MY SIN YOU CAN SEE:

_____

MY IDOL
UNDER THIS SIN:

I have **LOVE / TRUST / FEAR** of:
(CIRCLE ONE)

_____

I DON'T REALLY
BELIEVE GOD, THAT:

MY IDOL
UNDER THIS SIN:

I have **LOVE / TRUST / FEAR** of:
(CIRCLE ONE)

I DON'T REALLY
BELIEVE GOD, THAT:

MY IDOL
UNDER THIS SIN:

I have **LOVE / TRUST / FEAR** of:
(CIRCLE ONE)

I DON'T REALLY
BELIEVE GOD, THAT:

As you note your sin, remember that **IN JESUS YOU HAVE FORGIVENESS**, and that
HIS SPIRIT WILL WORK IN YOUR HEART to fix the big sin and the unbelief that lurks under the surface.
Use your time filling out this page as a time of confession and prayer.

THAT'S MY DAD!

Big Idea: Living as God's Child

BEFORE YOU BEGIN

Share something you learned about your sin this week.

What was a surface-level sin? _____

What idol in your life caused you to sin that way? _____

Your idol means there was something about Jesus you didn't believe.

What did you **not believe**?

_____

_____

_____

Did you experience any growth? By seeing your unbelief and praying about it, were you able to believe more deeply? Share about this.

TODAY'S LESSON

Sometimes it's hard to believe that Jesus is *so good* to you. It helps to remember that God is a great King and Jesus makes you the King's child.

Imagine a good and powerful king who rules a vast kingdom. He reigns from the largest, most dazzling castle in the world. For most people, just to visit that castle would be a breathtaking honor. To actually meet the king once and speak to him would fulfill the dream of a lifetime. To become his trusted advisor is impossible. It'll never happen.

But YOU are the king's child. He loves you with all his heart. You spend time with him whenever you want. For meals, you sit next to him in the castle's great banquet hall, eating at his table and talking with him about every need of the kingdom.

What <u>HONOR</u> is yours!

What <u>INFLUENCE</u> you have in the kingdom!

What <u>POWER</u> you have to do good in the world!

What <u>CONFIDENCE</u> you enjoy!

Best of all, what <u>LOVE</u> and <u>APPROVAL</u> you feel from the king himself, your dad!

In this lesson, you'll see how a believer's life with God is like that story.

PART 1: THE ORPHAN AND THE KING

Let's begin by learning about an orphan and a king in the Bible. First, meet the characters.

The King:
David

New king of Israel, living in a palace in Jerusalem

Became king after being hunted by the old king, Saul

Godly man who was friends with Saul's son, Jonathan, even though Saul was his enemy

- - - - - - - - - - - - - - - - - - -

The Orphan:
Mephibosheth (Meh-FIB-oh-sheth)

Grandson of Saul, living in disgrace in Lo-debar, on the outskirts of Israel

Crippled as a child when he fled the palace after his father and Saul were killed in battle

One of the few surviving members of the family of Saul, David's old enemy

Now read the story.

And David said, "Is there still anyone left of the house of Saul, that I may show him kindness for Jonathan's sake?"

Now there was a servant of the house of Saul whose name was Ziba, and they called him to David. Ziba said to the king, "There is still a son of Jonathan; he is crippled in his feet."

The king said to him, "Where is he?"

And Ziba said to the king, "He is in the house of Machir the son of Ammiel, at Lo-debar."

Then King David sent and brought him. And Mephibosheth the son of Jonathan, son of Saul, came to David and fell on his face and paid homage.

And David said, "Mephibosheth!"

And he answered, "Behold, I am your servant."

And David said to him, "Do not fear, for I will show you kindness for the sake of your father Jonathan, and I will restore to you all the land of Saul, and you shall eat at my table always."

Then the king called Ziba, Saul's servant, and said to him, "All that belonged to Saul and to all his house I have given to your master's grandson. And you and your sons and your servants shall till the land for him and shall bring in the produce, that your master's grandson may have bread to eat. But Mephibosheth your master's grandson shall always eat at my table."

So Mephibosheth ate at David's table, like one of the king's sons. And all who lived in Ziba's house became Mephibosheth's servants. So Mephibosheth lived in Jerusalem, for he ate always at the king's table. (excerpted from 2 Samuel 9)

How much did Mephibosheth <u>deserve</u> for David to be kind to him?

☐	☐	☐	☐	☐
Not at all	Only a little	Somewhat	Quite a bit	He totally earned it!

How great was David's kindness to Mephibosheth?

☐	☐	☐	☐	☐
Barely kind at all	A little bit kind	Somewhat kind	Very kind	Incredibly kind!

How do you think Mephibosheth felt at the end of the story compared to how he felt at the beginning?

Why do you think the Bible mentions *four times* how David let Mephibosheth always eat at the king's table? What's so important about that?

PART 2: YOUR FATHER THE KING

Mephibosheth was an orphan (his father had died). Then David—the king himself!—became like a father to him. That's a picture of what happens to you when you believe in Jesus. Even though you don't deserve it and have been a God-hating sinner, God <u>adopts you</u> as his child.

Look up the following verses in your Bible and fill in the blanks.

Galatians 3:26

For in

_____

you are all

_____ *through faith.*

John 1:12

But to all who did

_____ *who*

_____, *he gave the right to become*

_____.

The story of the good and powerful king who's your dad isn't just a fairy tale to imagine. It's all true! When God saves you, he does more than just forgive your sin and count you righteous. He also makes you his own son or daughter.

The list below includes some of the benefits of being a son or daughter. Next to each Bible verse, write the benefit it describes (some might describe more than one).

BENEFITS OF DAUGHTERS AND SONS:

1. **CARE:** Your father takes care of you and protects you.

2. **INHERITANCE:** You get a share of everything your father owns.

3. **LOVE:** Your father accepts you, enjoys spending time with you and listens to you.

4. **HONOR:** You share your father's name and reputation

Benefit

Verse

_____

You are no longer a slave, but a son, and if a son, then an heir through God. (Galatians 4:7)

_____

We know that he hears us in whatever we ask. (1 John 5:15)

_____

Let us then with confidence draw near to the throne of grace, that we may receive mercy and find grace to help in time of need. (Hebrews 4:16)

_____

Casting all your anxieties on him, because he cares for you. (1 Peter 5:7)

_____

Blessed are the meek, for they shall inherit the earth. (Matthew 5:5)

_____

Who shall separate us from the love of Christ? Shall tribulation, or distress, or persecution, or famine, or nakedness, or danger, or sword? (Romans 8:35)

See what kind of love the Father has given to us, that we should be called children of God; and so we are. (1 John 3:1)

_____

Let no one boast in men, for all things are yours. (1 Corinthians 3:21)

What are some ways that being a child of God ought to feel a lot like the story from the beginning of this lesson about you being a king's child? How would you compare it to that?

PART 3: LIVING LIKE A DAUGHTER OR SON

Let's compare an orphan with a child who has parents.

Orphan

Child who has parents

DISCUSS.

Which will be more scared? Why?

Which will worry about having to take care of himself? Why?

Which will always be trying to get people to like her? Why?

If you're joined to Jesus, God always loves you—even when you don't deserve it—because you're his child. But if you forget this *you* might start to act like an orphan.

❑ You might act scared.

❑ You might act like you need to look out for your own interests.

❑ You might act like you need to make people like you.

Each of these students has two ways they can think. One is "orphan thinking." The other is thinking like a son or daughter. For each student, put an X through the orphan thinking.

"I'm scared to talk about Jesus. It's too personal. I might say the wrong thing or get a strange look. I only do it if I absolutely have to."

"I'm eager to tell others about Jesus even if I don't always have the right words to say."

"I have brains. I'm talented. I'm good at sports. And I have nice clothes and a good house. These things make me special. I'm worth something."

"Only God satisfies my soul. I'm worth much because I'm his child."

TALK ABOUT IT

Look back at the past several pages and think more about the ways a son or daughter will act. Tell which of those examples are the hardest for you. Circle some orphan statements that sound like the way you often talk or think.

There's a responsibility that comes with being a child of the King. You need to act like your Dad. The Bible says those who are God's children keep his commandments, and "by this it is evident who are the children of God" (1 John 3:10). How much do you think you look and act like a child of God?

Imagine you absolutely believed everything the Bible tells you about being a child of the King. How would your thinking and your behavior be more like a daughter or son . . .

> . . . at home?

> . . . at school?

> . . . at church?

> . . . with your friends?

Before you finish this lesson, you need to know about the end of the Mephibosheth story.

Years later, King David had to flee Jerusalem when enemies attacked. People thought Mephibosheth, as a member of Saul's family, would side with the enemies while David was gone. David even gave Mephibosheth's land to Ziba.

But when David returned, he found Mephibosheth had been so sad he hadn't even washed himself the whole time. Then Mephibosheth explained why he was so devoted to David: "All my grandfather's descendants deserved nothing but death from my lord the king, but you gave your servant a place among those who eat at your table" (2 Samuel 19:28 NIV).

Mephibosheth knew he was undeserving but was made a son! He was grateful. It changed his behavior. And when David offered to make Ziba give up the land again, Mephibosheth said, "Let him take everything, now that my lord the king has returned home safely" (v. 30 NIV).

Mephibosheth didn't care about what David could give him. He just loved David himself!

PRAY ABOUT IT

You can have that kind of love for your Father and King too. You need to sit at his table. You need to enjoy being his honored child.

Finish this lesson by turning back to the verses that tell the benefits of being a child of God. Take turns praying, thanking your Father for everything mentioned in those verses. Then ask him to help you believe they're all true!

MAKE IT STICK:

THINK LIKE A SON OR DAUGHTER

INSTRUCTIONS:

☐ Fill out this Make It Stick page during the week.
☐ Don't forget to bring your *Student Guide* back next time you meet.
☐ If you have time, go ahead and get started now.

This chart compares thinking like an orphan with thinking like a son or daughter. Read how an orphan thinks and then look up and read the verse that tells how a son or daughter of God thinks. In your own words, finish filling in the chart by writing how a son or daughter of God thinks.

HOW AN ORPHAN THINKS	WHAT GOD SAYS	HOW A SON OR DAUGHTER OF GOD THINKS
If only I could run faster, be taller, be thinner, or be as smart as he/she is, then I'd be accepted. It isn't fair!	John 1:12	My self-worth comes from . . .
I make sure I pray every day. It's the only way to keep God happy with me.	Psalm 16:11	I pray because . . .
No one understands me and what I want. No one loves me.	1 John 4:16	I believe that . . .
I go to church and pray and study the Bible but it's mostly so other people will see and approve.	Psalm 122:1	I go to church because . . .
If I get good grades, or have good friends, or keep a good attitude my life will be better.	Psalm 84:11–12	God is in control of my life. I believe that he will . . .
I need to please everyone—my parents, my friends, my teachers . . .	1 Thessalonians 2:4	I can't please everyone. Instead I . . .
God can't help me. I don't want to hear about him.	Isaiah 58:11	I trust that God can and will . . .
I must not fail! If I can't win I won't even try!	Philippians 4:12–13	It's okay to try and fail or to be weak. I can take it because . . .
People are always so mean! They pick on me. They aren't fair.	Philippians 4:6–8	People are mean (and I am too sometimes) but . . .
I don't like my house. I don't like my friends. I don't like my hair. I don't like my life . . .	Romans 8:28	I trust that God is . . .

When you finish, pick one place from the chart where you want to think less like an orphan and more like a son or daughter of God. Circle it. As you pray this week, thank God for how you're a daughter or son and ask him to help you to believe it and live like what you circled.

GRR...THAT MAKES ME SO MAD!

Big Idea: Resolving Conflicts

BEFORE YOU BEGIN

From the last lesson share one place where you want to think less like an orphan and more like a son or daughter of God. Write that orphan thinking and son/daughter thinking on the lines below.

Orphan thinking _____

Son/daughter of God thinking _____

Share how you sometimes behave like an orphan. Then explain how it helps to believe that you're part of God's family. (HINT: Remember that God's children have <u>care</u>, an <u>inheritance</u>, <u>honor,</u> and <u>love</u> from God.)

TODAY'S LESSON

Raise your hand if you've ever been in an argument with someone.

If you raised your hand, this lesson is for you. We're going to learn about arguments and conflicts. Let's start with a little quiz, just to see what you already think about conflicts.

Write TRUE or FALSE by each statement. Then discuss your answers, if you'd like.

_____ Conflicts start in my heart.

_____ I should treat others the same way they treat me.

_____ I should pray for those who are kind to me, but not for those who are mean to me.

_____ I need the Holy Spirit to help me love my enemies.

_____ I need to forgive others if I'm going to love them.

_____ I can overcome evil by being evil back.

_____ It's okay for me to pretend to be nice to someone, then talk badly about them behind their backs (they deserve it anyway—they're really mean!).

_____ Loving someone means I never have any conflict with them.

In this lesson, you'll start by learning where your conflicts come from. Then, in part 2, you'll see how being a child of God can help you solve conflicts.

PART 1: WHERE CONFLICTS COME FROM

Do you know the story of Joseph and his older brothers? Joseph's father loved him more than the others. God also gave Joseph dreams that said he'd become great. The Bible says, "his brothers were jealous of him" (Genesis 37:11).

Read **Genesis 37:12–26** to see what their anger and jealousy led to. Then, match the right surface sin to each blank.

Joseph's brothers _____ to kill him. They _____ him and

_____ him into a pit. They _____ him of his beautiful robe. Then they

_____ him as a slave to some traders. The traders took Joseph from his father's homeland to

Egypt. The brothers _____ to their father and said Joseph was dead.

WORD LIST:
sold   plotted   lied   threw   grabbed   stripped

Notice how the behavior of Joseph's brothers started with anger and jealousy in their hearts. The anger and jealousy grew in them until they made some terrible, mean choices.

Now read **James 4:1–2**.

What causes fights and quarrels among you? Don't they come from your desires that battle within you? You want something but don't get it. You kill and covet, but you cannot have what you want. You quarrel and fight. (NIV)

According to this verse, where do conflicts come from?

_____

Circle the words "desires" and "want" and "covet" in the verse. We have desires and things we covet. Our hearts WANT something. When we can't have it, we get mad. We treat others badly.

Each student below WANTS something that results in them being angry or treating others badly. Match what each student wants with what they're feeling in their heart.

"I want to be right. I can't stand being wrong! When my mom or dad corrects me, I get defensive and argue with them about it."

_____

"I want a better life. No one likes me at school. I don't have any friends because I have so much homework. My life is awful!"

_____

LIST OF HEART CONDITIONS:

Jealousy
Greed & envy
Pride
Fear of others
Selfishness
Anger
Self-pity

"I want revenge. If someone hurts me or embarrasses me, it makes me want to do something even worse to them. I won't rest until I get them back and I won't be nice to them!"

"I want my friends to approve of me. Last week my friend wanted to take something that wasn't hers. I might have helped her by telling her not to, but I was afraid she wouldn't like me if I disagreed. I'm even more afraid to tell her about Jesus. Who knows what she might think?!"

LIST OF HEART CONDITIONS:

Jealousy
Greed & envy
Pride
Fear of others
Selfishness
Anger
Self-pity

TALK ABOUT IT

Are you like any of those students? What things do *you* want that lead you to treat others badly— and end up in conflict? Give an example of when that's happened.

The next part of this lesson will explain what you can do to resolve conflicts. But by now, you've been studying *What's Up?* long enough that you might have some good ideas without having to be told. So before you start part 2, think: what have you learned in past lessons that might help you fix conflict when it happens? Write down your answer and share it with the group.

PART 2: HOW CONFLICTS ARE RESOLVED

When you treat others badly, it shows you have a problem in your heart. Your surface sin comes from things you want—idols—in your heart! Do you remember what you can do about idols in your heart? (HINT: Think ocean, dorsal fin, and razor-sharp teeth.)

REVIEW

The SHARK taught you that surface sins (like treating others badly) come from idols in your heart. You learned to do two things about that:

1. You learned to <u>believe</u> all that God gives you in Jesus. Jesus is better than your idols. You've especially learned to believe that God is your loving, caring Father—so you'll act like a son or daughter.

2. You learned to <u>trust the Holy Spirit</u> by praying and spending time in God's Word. The Spirit helps you fight sin and believe.

What about the conflicts Joseph had in his life? Did *he* do those two things? Did he believe and trust God? He did!

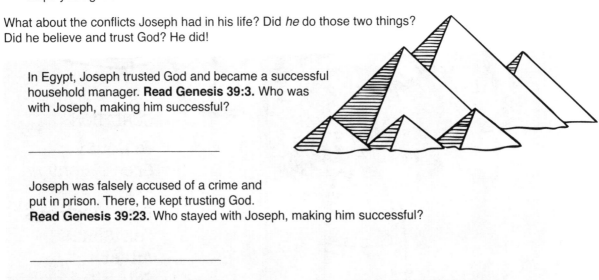

In Egypt, Joseph trusted God and became a successful household manager. **Read Genesis 39:3.** Who was with Joseph, making him successful?

_____

Joseph was falsely accused of a crime and put in prison. There, he kept trusting God. **Read Genesis 39:23.** Who stayed with Joseph, making him successful?

_____

Finally, Joseph got a chance to interpret a dream for the Pharaoh. He was put in charge of the whole country of Egypt. He stored up food and was able to save many people from starving when a terrible famine came. **Read Genesis 41:38.** Who was Joseph's helper, working with him and in him to make him so successful?

_____

During the famine Joseph's brothers went to Egypt to buy food. Joseph remembered how they'd harmed him. What would *he* do to *them* now that he was in charge and had the food they needed?

Well, Joseph gave them free food. He wept with joy. He told them who he was and said not to worry:

> "I am your brother Joseph, the one you sold into Egypt! And now, do not be distressed and do not be angry with yourselves for selling me here, because it was to save lives that God sent me ahead of you." (Genesis 45:4–5 NIV)

Later, his brothers asked Joseph to forgive them. He wept again and spoke to them more:

> Joseph said to them, "Don't be afraid. Am I in the place of God? You intended to harm me, but God intended it for good to accomplish what is now being done, the saving of many lives. So then, don't be afraid. I will provide for you and your children." And he reassured them and spoke kindly to them. (Genesis 50:19–21 NIV)

Check the statements you think are TRUE REASONS why Joseph could be kind to his brothers even though they'd been so mean to him.

❑ Joseph understood and believed that God had been very kind to him, so in his heart he was able to be kind to others.

❑ Joseph believed in God's saving work. This was more wonderful and important to him than what others had done to him.

❑ Joseph tried very hard to be nice even though he was angry. It worked because he was an especially nice guy.

❑ Joseph decided it was easier to forget what had happened and just pretend his brothers hadn't been so mean.

❑ Joseph believed that God had loved him and cared for him like a Father. This mattered more to him than how his brothers treated him.

❑ Joseph did everything by working together with God's Spirit, who was always with him and in him, helping him to behave like a child of God.

TALK ABOUT IT

How did Joseph act like a son of God instead of like an orphan? (If necessary, review the lists in the last lesson that compare the thinking of orphans and sons/daughters. Pick some of the son/daughter items that fit Joseph's forgiveness of his brothers.)

Because of Jesus, you can be like Joseph too!

<u>Jesus saves you</u> from sin and death. That's even better than being saved from famine. Believing God's kindness to you will help you want to be kind to others.

<u>Jesus gives you</u> the Holy Spirit to always be with you and in you. You have the same power Joseph had to act like a child of your heavenly Father.

Because you're the son or daughter of such a great Father, the Bible gives you some radical instructions about how to deal with conflicts. Read what it says:

"You have heard that it was said, 'You shall love your neighbor and hate your enemy.' But I say to you, Love your enemies and pray for those who persecute you, so that you may be sons of your Father who is in heaven." (Matthew 5:43–45)

Repay no one evil for evil. . . . To the contrary, "if your enemy is hungry, feed him; if he is thirsty, give him something to drink; for by so doing you will heap burning coals on his head." Do not be overcome by evil, but overcome evil with good. (Romans 12:17, 20–21)

Let all bitterness and wrath and anger and clamor and slander be put away from you, along with all malice. Be kind to one another, tenderhearted, forgiving one another, as God in Christ forgave you. (Ephesians 4:31–32)

Circle four things these verses say to do for your enemies and those who hurt you.

You can't overcome evil by being evil. Underline how a child of God *can* overcome evil.

★Put a star by the reason why you should forgive those who do wrong to you.

It's hard to love others well—especially when there's conflict! It starts with forgiving others as God forgave you. It might also mean doing something nice for others or going to them and talking to them about the conflict. This could be SCARY. But God and the gospel help us to do it.

Sin means you get hurt and hurt others. But God is saving you from sin. His Spirit helps you love others, even when someone's been mean.

Point to remember:
When you fight sin, don't try to do it by yourself.
Do it by trusting God.

PRAY ABOUT IT

You've already trusted God by reading his Word. Now trust him more by praying. You can pray in a group or write your prayer below. Pray for three things:

1. Pray that God would help you believe his goodness and act like his son or daughter.

2. Pray that God would make you kind to people who are mean to you.

3. Pray that God would make you brave to talk to people you're mad at and fix conflicts.

End by looking again at these statements about conflicts. This time, circle the words that make these statements correct.

- **Conflicts start IN MY HEART / WITH SOMEONE BEING MEAN.**

- **I should treat others THE SAME WAY THEY TREAT ME / WITH LOVE.**

- **I should pray for those who are kind to me, BUT NOT / AND for those who are mean to me.**

- **I need THE HOLY SPIRIT / MORE SELF-EFFORT to help me love my enemies.**

- **I NEED / DON'T NEED to forgive others if I'm going to love them.**

- **I can overcome evil BY BEING EVIL BACK / WITH GOOD.**

- **It's OKAY / NOT OKAY for me to pretend to be nice to someone, then talk badly about them behind their backs (they deserve it anyway—they're really mean!).**

- **Loving someone means I NEVER HAVE ANY CONFLICT WITH THEM / FIX MY CONFLICTS WITH THEM.**

MAKE IT STICK:

THE ORPHANS VS. SONS/DAUGHTERS FIGURE

INSTRUCTIONS:

- ❑ Fill out this Make It Stick page during the week.
- ❑ Don't forget to bring your *Student Guide* back next time you meet.
- ❑ If you have time, go ahead and get started now.

Think of a person you struggle to get along with. This week's assignment is to pray for *that person* at least four times—yes, do it AGAIN and AGAIN and AGAIN.

When you pray, ask God to do four things:

1. Ask God to help you forgive the person for ways they've hurt you.

2. Ask God to show you some ways you can be kind to that person and love them.

3. Ask God to make you brave to do those kind things, remembering how he is kind to you.

4. Think of a specific thing that would be nice or helpful to that person, and ask God to do it for them.

To get started, take a moment right now to pray for the person. Use the Praying for Someone checklist to keep track of the rest of your praying this week.

PRAYING FOR SOMEONE

Directions: Think of a person you have trouble getting along with. You will pray for that person *four times.* Pick a time of day to do it. (If you miss your time, you can still pray later, but try to remember.)

I will pray for this person at _____ for four days.
(time of day)

Now use this checklist to keep a record of your daily prayers.

DAY ONE
- ☐ I asked God to help me forgive the person for ways they've hurt me.
- ☐ I asked God to show me ways to be kind to that person.
  (If he *did* show you a way to be kind, write that way here.) _____
- ☐ I asked God to make me brave to do that kind thing, remembering how kind God is to me.
- ☐ I asked God for a specific thing he would do to be nice or helpful to that person.

The specific thing I asked God to do today was _____.

DAY TWO
- ☐ I asked God to help me forgive the person for ways they've hurt me.
- ☐ I asked God to show me ways to be kind to that person.
  (If he *did* show you a way to be kind, write that way here.) _____
- ☐ I asked God to make me brave to do that kind thing, remembering how kind God is to me.
- ☐ I asked God for a specific thing he would do to be nice or helpful to that person.

The specific thing I asked God to do today was _____.

DAY THREE
- ☐ I asked God to help me forgive the person for ways they've hurt me.
- ☐ I asked God to show me ways to be kind to that person.
  (If he *did* show you a way to be kind, write that way here.) _____
- ☐ I asked God to make me brave to do that kind thing, remembering how kind God is to me.
- ☐ I asked God for a specific thing he would do to be nice or helpful to that person.

The specific thing I asked God to do today was _____.

DAY FOUR
- ☐ I asked God to help me forgive the person for ways they've hurt me.
- ☐ I asked God to show me ways to be kind to that person.
  (If he *did* show you a way to be kind, write that way here.) _____
- ☐ I asked God to make me brave to do that kind thing, remembering how kind God is to me.
- ☐ I asked God for a specific thing he would do to be nice or helpful to that person.

The specific thing I asked God to do today was _____.

I'M SO SORRY—NOT!

Big Idea: False Repentance

BEFORE YOU BEGIN

Talk about your assignment from last time to pray for someone you have trouble getting along with. What was good about it?

You probably noticed that the assignment included asking God to make you brave to love that person and be kind to them—but you weren't assigned to actually *do* any nice things or say something to that person. If praying did lead you to do something kind, that's great! But what did you think of an assignment to <u>pray</u> about something instead of an assignment to <u>do</u> something?

What do you think might be some good reasons for an assignment to <u>pray</u> instead of an assignment to <u>do</u>? Discuss.

TODAY'S LESSON

Sometimes you might try to do something good <u>for</u> God—but forget to do it <u>with</u> God. You forget to trust him for help. He's on your side! He works in you.

So it's good for you to be kind to the person you prayed for, but you needed to pray first. That helps you do it *with God* instead of . . .

. . . to feel proud about yourself.

OR

. . . to prove to God how good you are.

OR

. . . just so life will go better for you.

In today's lesson, you'll learn how working *with God* is important whenever you repent of sin.

PART 1: TWO WAYS TO BE SORRY

In this section, you'll learn how there's a difference between being sorry about what happened when you sinned and being truly sorry for the sin itself.

Read this story. It's a real story that happened to one of the authors of this lesson.

The young teacher stood on the playground. It was the second day of school and so far things had gone well. But then she noticed two of her second graders were rolling on the ground. A small crowd of students began to form around the two boys. They were fighting. She rushed over and called out for the boys to stop. They were so engrossed in punching each other, they didn't hear their teacher. Finally, she took each boy by his collar and pulled them apart. They were covered in grass and dirt with sweat running down their faces. In her anger, the teacher yelled, "You both apologize to one another right now!" Glaring at one another, both boys clenched their teeth and practically growled, " I'm sorry."

From the story above, do you think the two boys really were sorry for hurting each other? What clues do you have that, although they stopped fighting, they didn't really repent the way God wants?

Look up **2 Corinthians 7:10**. Fill in the blanks to see what the Bible says about two kinds of being sorry.

<u>Godly sorrow</u> (or grief) brings

_____

and leads to

_____.

But <u>worldly sorrow</u> brings

_____.

GODLY SORROW
is being <u>Sorry for your Sin</u>.

WORLDLY SORROW
is being <u>Sorry for what happened to you</u> because of your Sin, like . . .

- ❏ Sorry you got caught

- ❏ Sorry you feel guilty

- ❏ Sorry you had bad consequences

- ❏ Sorry you might have made God mad at you

- ❏ Sorry you don't feel good about yourself

GODLY SORROW
means you hate Sin like God does.

WORLDLY SORROW
means you still wish you could get away with your Sin, even if you've decided to stop doing it.

These students all have ideas about repentance. Circle the ones you think are right ideas about the kind of being sorry God wants. Then tell why you think they're right—or not.

"I cheated on a test and got caught. It turned out very badly for me. Boy, am I sorry I ever cheated. I've learned my lesson. No more cheating for me! I've repented."

"I lied to my mom. She didn't catch me, but now I feel SO guilty about it. I need to make sure I never do that again. It's feels horrible! I've repented."

TALK ABOUT IT

False repentance is VERY common. Give some more examples you can think of.

PART 2: IDENTIFYING FALSE REPENTANCE

Now see if you can tell what's wrong in some examples of false repentance in the Bible.

NOT real repentance example:
King Saul

God told King Saul to fight the evil Amalekites and kill all the people and their animals. Saul fought them, but decided to keep some alive. God's prophet Samuel went to scold Saul for disobeying God.

Saul made excuses. He said, "I did *most* of what God told me. It was the people—not me—who didn't want to follow God's instructions. We only kept some animals so we could offer them as sacrifices to God."

But Samuel saw that Saul's heart was against obeying God. He said God wouldn't let Saul keep being king. Samuel also refused to honor Saul by travelling home with him. When Saul saw that his excuses weren't working, he decided to say he was sorry. Read what he said:

> "I have sinned. I violated the LORD's command and your instructions. I was afraid of the people and so I gave in to them. . . . But please honor me before the elders of my people and before Israel; come back with me." (1 Samuel 15:24, 30 NIV)

<u>Underline</u> the words Saul said that sound like repentance.

Now think of at least three ways you can tell Saul wasn't really sorry for his sin even though he said some good-sounding things.

1. _____

2. _____

3. _____

TALK ABOUT IT

Give an example of a sin someone your age might be caught doing. In that situation, how might you be tempted to make excuses or say you're sorry just to avoid bad consequences instead of repenting in your heart? Share your example with the group, or write the false repentance words you might say.

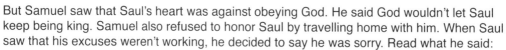

NOT real repentance example:
Judas

Judas was one of Jesus's disciples. He did a horrible thing. He betrayed Jesus by telling people who wanted to kill him how best to arrest him. He got paid thirty pieces of silver for it. Jesus was arrested, put on trial, and killed.

After the trial, Judas felt guilty. He was so sorry about what happened that he tried to give the silver pieces back to Jesus's enemies. Read what happened:

> Then when Judas, his betrayer, saw that Jesus was condemned, he changed his mind and brought back the thirty pieces of silver to the chief priests and the elders, saying, "I have sinned by betraying innocent blood." They said, "What is that to us? See to it yourself." And throwing down the pieces of silver into the temple, he departed, and he went and hanged himself. (Matthew 27:3–5)

Underline the parts of the passage that show how Judas felt guilty and sorry about the way his evil plan turned out.

But which kind of sorrow did Judas have?

_____ A godly sorrow that leads to salvation

_____ A worldly sorrow that brings death

Judas never repented of being greedy for money and hating Jesus in his heart. He was just trying to get rid of his guilty feelings. What things did he do that show he was only trying to make himself feel better?

TALK ABOUT IT

Give an example of a sin someone your age might do and then feel guilty about. In that situation, what things might you do instead of repenting in your heart—just to feel less guilty?

NOT real repentance example:
People of Judah and Israel

The leaders and shopkeepers in the countries of Judah and Israel were enjoying good times. They were getting rich. But they were doing it by cheating the poor people and taking land that wasn't theirs. They also worshiped idols.

They knew they were sinning, but they thought they could get away with it if they also did some things for God, like give him offerings.

God sent his prophet Micah to say this to them:

> *What can we bring to the LORD?*
> > *What kind of offerings should we give him?*
> *Should we bow before God*
> > *with offerings of yearling calves?*
> *Should we offer him thousands of rams*
> > *and ten thousand rivers of olive oil?*
> *Should we sacrifice our firstborn children*
> > *to pay for our sins?*
>
> *No, O people, the LORD has told you what is good,*
> > *and this is what he requires of you:*
> *To do what is right, to love mercy,*
> > *and to walk humbly with your God. (Micah 6:6–8 NLT)*

Underline the things the people offered to do for God to make up for their sin. Then circle the kind of repentance God really required.

Now think of at least three ways (more if you can) that the people's wrong repentance was different from the right repentance God required. Share your answers with the group and talk about them.

1. _____

2. _____

3. _____

The things those people offered to do for God sound WAY too extreme, don't they? Isn't it amazing how they would rather do *anything else* than truly repent in their hearts?

Sin is like that. It can make you think you would rather do *anything else* than repent in your heart. That's why you do wrong repentance instead.

CONCLUSION

Godly repentance is HARD. You'll never do it without God's help. You need to work with God to repent.

Read 1 John 3:9–10. Fill in what it says about sons and daughters of the Father:

"No one born of God makes a practice of

_____, for God's seed abides in him, and he cannot keep on

_____ because he has been

_____. By this it is evident who are the

_____ of God."

PRAY ABOUT IT

Finish by praying that God would make that verse true in your life. Pray as a group or write out your prayer below.

1. Thank God that his Spirit is in you, helping you to repent.

2. Pray that you would deeply believe that you are a child of your loving Father.

3. Pray that you would stop wrong repentance and be able to repent in your heart.

MAKE IT STICK:

HOW I RESPOND TO CORRECTION

INSTRUCTIONS:

- ❑ Fill out this Make It Stick page during the week.
- ❑ Don't forget to bring your *Student Guide* back next time you meet.
- ❑ If you have time, go ahead and get started now.

Godly repentance honors God and brings deep joy. You'll learn more about it next time. Spend the coming week noticing how you usually respond when your parents or someone else (like a teacher) correct you. Godly repentance is the best response, but be honest. If you do something else, it's good to notice that so you can confess it to God and work on it with his help.

HERE'S YOUR ASSIGNMENT:

1. Notice a few times in the coming week when you are corrected.

2. On the "How I Respond to Correction" table, write down what you did that needed correction.

3. Then check how you responded when you were corrected.

4. Be prepared to discuss your results next time.

WHOOPS! MY BAD.

How Do I Respond to Correction?

I WAS CORRECTED ABOUT:

_____

_____

_____

I RESPONDED BY:

HIDING MY SIN

- ❑ "I didn't do that."
- ❑ "You misunderstood me."
- ❑ "It looked worse than it really was."
- ❑ "You're being unfair!"

MAKING EXCUSES

- ❑ "Someone else started it."
- ❑ "I couldn't help it. I was tired, hungry, angry…"
- ❑ "I did good things too. Doesn't that count?"
- ❑ "You did something wrong too."

FALSE REPENTING

- ❑ "I'll change because I have no choice."
- ❑ "I'll change to show you I can be good."
- ❑ "I'll change so I won't feel guilty anymore."
- ❑ "I'll change … but no more than I have to."
- ❑ "I'm sorry it turned out this way for me."
- ❑ "I'm sorry you feel the way you do."

TRUE REPENTING

- ❑ "I'm sorry in my heart for my sin."

I WAS CORRECTED ABOUT:

_____

_____

_____

I RESPONDED BY:

HIDING MY SIN

- ❑ "I didn't do that."
- ❑ "You misunderstood me."
- ❑ "It looked worse than it really was."
- ❑ "You're being unfair!"

MAKING EXCUSES

- ❑ "Someone else started it."
- ❑ "I couldn't help it. I was tired, hungry, angry…"
- ❑ "I did good things too. Doesn't that count?"
- ❑ "You did something wrong too."

FALSE REPENTING

- ❑ "I'll change because I have no choice."
- ❑ "I'll change to show you I can be good."
- ❑ "I'll change so I won't feel guilty anymore."
- ❑ "I'll change … but no more than I have to."
- ❑ "I'm sorry it turned out this way for me."
- ❑ "I'm sorry you feel the way you do."

TRUE REPENTING

- ❑ "I'm sorry in my heart for my sin."

I WAS CORRECTED ABOUT:

_____

_____

_____

I RESPONDED BY:

HIDING MY SIN

- ❑ "I didn't do that."
- ❑ "You misunderstood me."
- ❑ "It looked worse than it really was."
- ❑ "You're being unfair!"

MAKING EXCUSES

- ❑ "Someone else started it."
- ❑ "I couldn't help it. I was tired, hungry, angry…"
- ❑ "I did good things too. Doesn't that count?"
- ❑ "You did something wrong too."

FALSE REPENTING

- ❑ "I'll change because I have no choice."
- ❑ "I'll change to show you I can be good."
- ❑ "I'll change so I won't feel guilty anymore."
- ❑ "I'll change … but no more than I have to."
- ❑ "I'm sorry it turned out this way for me."
- ❑ "I'm sorry you feel the way you do."

TRUE REPENTING

- ❑ "I'm sorry in my heart for my sin."

I'M SO SORRY—REALLY!

Big Idea: Godly Repentance

BEFORE YOU BEGIN

Share your results from the "How I Respond to Correction" chart. How did people try to correct you this week? How did you catch yourself responding to them?

What did you learn about your habits? Do you usually use being corrected as an opportunity to repent? Or have you gotten used to certain ways of avoiding repentance or practicing false repentance?

TODAY'S LESSON

Now that you're aware of false repentance, it's time to learn about more about godly repentance. First, you'll learn what it looks like. Then you'll learn what makes it so sweet.

To get started, check the statements you think sound like godly repentance. Then turn the page to begin.

_____ You **see** and admit the sin in your heart, not just the surface sins you do, with no excuses.

_____ You're **sorry** for your sin because it's horrible to God, not just because it turned out badly for you.

_____ You have a broken heart that's **sad** and ashamed at how you treated your heavenly Father.

_____ You **stop** doing *all* kinds of sin you see, not just a few sins you don't mind giving up.

PART 1: GODLY REPENTANCE— WHAT IS IT?

If you checked ALL of those statements, you're right. All of them are part of godly repentance. Let's look at an example of godly repentance in the Bible.

Real repentance example: King David

Kind David wanted the wife of one of his most loyal soldiers, Uriah. So he brought her to his palace and behaved with her like she was his wife. Then to hide that sin, David got rid of Uriah. He ordered that Uriah be put in a dangerous place in battle and abandoned there—to be killed. Once Uriah was dead, David married his wife.

Those were terrible sins and David had bad consequences from them. But God helped him to see how horrible they were, and David repented. He wrote about his repentance in Psalm 51. Read some of the things he said in his prayer to God:

> For I know my transgressions,
>   and my sin is always before me.
> Against you, you only, have I sinned
>   and done what is evil in your sight,
> so that you are proved right when you speak
>   and justified when you judge.
> Create in me a pure heart, O God,
>   and renew a steadfast spirit within me.
> The sacrifices of God are a broken spirit;
>   a broken and contrite heart,
>   O God, you will not despise. (Psalm 51:3–4, 10, 17 NIV)

<u>**Underline**</u> some parts that show David was concerned with his heart, not just surface sins.

Circle a part that shows David wasn't making any excuses.

 Put a star next to a part that shows David was sorry because his sin was horrible to God, not just for the consequences.

 Put a sad face next to a part that shows David had a broken heart that was sad and ashamed.

 Put a smiley face next to a part that shows David was willing to turn and live for God with his whole heart.

Real repentance example:
The Younger Son

Jesus taught about godly repentance, too, in his parable of the two sons that you studied in Lesson 6. In Jesus's story, the younger son asked his father for the family money he'd get when the father died. Then he left home and wasted the money in wild living. When it was gone, he was hungry and had to feed pigs. Read the rest of the story.

When he came to his senses, he said, "How many of my father's hired servants have food to spare, and here I am starving to death! I will set out and go back to my father and say to him: Father, I have sinned against heaven and against you. I am no longer worthy to be called your son; make me like one of your hired servants." So he got up and went to his father.

But while he was still a long way off, his father saw him and was filled with compassion for him; he ran to his son, threw his arms around him and kissed him.

The son said to him, "Father, I have sinned against heaven and against you. I am no longer worthy to be called your son."

But the father said to his servants, "Quick! Bring the best robe and put it on him. Put a ring on his finger and sandals on his feet. Bring the fattened calf and kill it. Let's have a feast and celebrate. For this son of mine was dead and is alive again; he was lost and is found." So they began to celebrate. (Luke 15:17–24 NIV)

<u>Underline</u> the parts that show the son was sorry because his sin was horrible to his father and to God, not because of the consequences to himself.

Put a squiggly line under the parts that show the son was heartbroken and ashamed by his sin and no longer proud or demanding.

Is the son repenting for what he'll get out of it, or is his selfishness gone? How can you tell?

Now draw a picture of what you think the son looked like when he repented to his father. What does his face look like? What's he doing with the rest of his body? Draw your picture below.

Explain to the rest of the group what you put in your picture of the son. What about it shows godly repentance?

Imagine you could read the thoughts of students when they have an opportunity to repent. Some would be NOT SORRY. Others would be REALLY SORRY. Here are some students and the two ways each might think.

TALK ABOUT IT

Which NOT SORRY and REALLY SORRY ways of thinking sound the most like your own life? Circle three places that sound like ways you tend to be NOT SORRY, or that sound like ways you're becoming more REALLY SORRY. Give an example from your life that fits something you circled.

PART 2: GODLY REPENTANCE— WHY DO IT?

Does godly repentance seem too hard? Well, you have to do it while *working with God*. Jesus said to remain in him: "Apart from me you can do nothing" (John 15:5).

Start by remembering how much your Father loves you because of Jesus. When you confess your sin to him, he won't scold you. He *loves* to welcome you. He's eager to help you.

When you come to him to repent, God acts toward you like the father in Jesus's story acted toward the younger son. So go back a few pages to that story. Put a big smiley face by every place you can find that shows how much the father loves the son—even though that son has been sinning.

Now, like you drew a picture of the son, draw a picture of how you think the father looked while the son was confessing and repenting. What does *his* face look like? What's *he* doing with his body? Draw your picture below.

Show your picture to the group. Tell what you put in your picture that fits how God welcomes you when you come to him in repentance.

JUST THINK . . .

- ❑ Sin is the most hideous evil and the filthiest thing about you—and you're getting rid of it!

- ❑ You're coming closer to your Father who loves you!

- ❑ You're serving Jesus! There's no one and nothing better.

- ❑ When you repent you're like the younger son, greeted with honor and celebration and a humungous hug. There's joy in heaven!

- ❑ Your sin is shameful, but repenting has *nothing* to be ashamed about. It's God-honoring and noble—the *very best* thing you could do today!

- ❑ God is *so* kind to you that you're joined to Jesus, forgiven, and allowed to repent!

ARE YOU THINKING, *DIDN'T I DO THIS?*

Does this lesson seem a lot like Lesson 6, when you imagined what the father was thinking and wrote it out? That's on purpose! It's because remembering God's love for you, a sinner, is something you need to keep doing— again and again. Never forget how Jesus died for you and God welcomes you as an eager Father—or else you'll never cry over your sin or want to repent.

Godly repentance is SWEET! There's sadness involved, and much struggling. But the end result is great joy.

PRAY ABOUT IT

Pray now with your group. Do three things when you pray:

1. Thank God. Pick some of the great things about repentance mentioned above that make you most eager to repent. Underline the ones you picked, and then thank God for them. You can also pick something about your picture of the Father and thank God for that.

2. Ask God to make your heart eager to repent. Pray with confidence in the Holy Spirit. He's on your side and lives in you to do exactly what you're asking!

3. Ask God to bless you with repentance. You might need to pray about specific sins you know you need to repent of. Ask God to help you give them up and turn to him. (If the sins you need to repent of aren't appropriate to share with the group, you can pray this part silently or write out your prayer.)

MAKE IT STICK:

KEEP PRAYING FOR REPENTANCE

INSTRUCTIONS:

- ❑ Fill out this Make It Stick page during the week.
- ❑ Don't forget to bring your *Student Guide* back next time you meet.
- ❑ If you have time, go ahead and get started now.

Look back at the examples from your life that you circled in the list of NOT SORRY and REALLY SORRY ways to think about repentance. Write the REALLY SORRY side of those examples here.

1. _____

2. _____

3. _____

This week when you pray, ask God to:

- ❑ Make you more REALLY SORRY in the ways you wrote down.

- ❑ Help you to notice when you're NOT SORRY and when you're REALLY SORRY.

Put a check mark by each REALLY SORRY way of thinking every time you pray about it this week.

I (GULP) FORGIVE YOU

Big Idea: Forgiving Others

BEFORE YOU BEGIN

Talk about last time's assignment to pray that you'd notice when you're NOT SORRY and when you're REALLY SORRY. What did you notice about how you usually think? Share an example of a time when you noticed yourself behaving in one of those ways.

Sometimes people get so used to NOT SORRY thinking that it gets very hard to be REALLY SORRY. Do you think that's happened with you? Did you remember to pray to God and keep asking him to bless you with true repentance?

TODAY'S LESSON

Remember that you'll never *want* to repent and obey God unless you know HOW MUCH he's already forgiven you. In this lesson, you'll learn how your heavenly Father's forgiveness also makes you able to forgive others.

First you'll learn *why* you ought to forgive. Then you'll learn *how much* you ought to forgive.

PART 1: WHY SHOULD I FORGIVE?

Read the story, *The Board that Soared*.

The Board that Soared

Ethan loved his skateboard. His family was poor, but Ethan had saved enough money to buy the board. He rode it everywhere—that is, everywhere except down the walkway to the neighbor Mrs. Vincent's driveway and flower garden. Mrs. Vincent was poor too. Ethan knew she barely had enough money to put gas in her old car, drive to the store, and buy groceries for herself and seeds for her much-loved garden. His dad had warned him many times never to ride his skateboard down the walkway. "You might lose control and land in Mrs. Vincent's flowers—or worse," he told him.

One day Ethan decided he just HAD to try the walkway on his board.

I can make it! Besides, who cares about those stupid flowers anyway?

Whoops!

The board flew right into the windshield of Mrs. Vincent's car!

The windshield would have to be replaced. It'd cost hundreds of dollars.

His dad told him they didn't have the money to pay for the damage and that Ethan would have to work every Saturday until he could pay Mrs. Vincent for a new windshield. He even suggested that Ethan sell his skateboard in order to pay her back!

It's okay, Ethan. I guess I'll walk to the store until I can save enough money for a new windshield. You don't have to pay me anything.

I'm so sorry, Mrs. Vincent. I know I can't pay you, but please don't make me work or sell my skateboard!

Ethan was so grateful that he couldn't stop thanking Mrs. Vincent for her kindness.

The next day Ethan came home from school to find his sister Sarah riding his skateboard.

As he watched, it slipped from under her and landed on a rock. The skateboard got badly scratched.

TALK ABOUT IT

Share with the group what you wrote for Ethan to say. Also tell what you think he *should* say.

Do you think Ethan's experience the day before with Mrs. Vincent should make him MORE LIKELY or LESS LIKELY to forgive his sister? Why?

The story about Ethan is like a story Jesus told. Read Jesus's story in **Matthew 18:23–35**.

Why was the master right to be so angry with the servant who wouldn't forgive? Discuss.

In both stories, someone was **forgiven**.

Forgiveness:
Not counting what someone owes you, or how they hurt you, against them anymore even though they still deserve it.

Think about that. Forgiveness makes little sense. Why would you decide to not count what someone owed you or how they hurt you—*unless you'd been forgiven too?!*

Jesus told his story to make you think of how God has forgiven you. If you realize how being forgiven by God is THE VERY BEST THING that's ever happened in your life, then you'll want to forgive others too. Then it makes sense.

Point to remember:
When you treasure how God forgives you, you'll also forgive others.

The Bible says being forgiven by God means you forgive others.
Fill in the blanks to complete these verses.

Colossians 3:13. As the Lord has forgiven you, so you also must _____.

Mark 11:25. Whenever you stand praying, forgive, if you have anything against anyone,

so that your _____ also who is in heaven may forgive you.

Now look at those two verses. The first one says that you should forgive because God forgave you. But the second one says something a bit different. Tell how it's different.

The Bible says forgiving others is part of being forgiven by God. They go together so much that if you don't forgive, you shouldn't think God is really forgiving you. If you really know how big a sinner you are and how much God forgives you, it *will* make you forgive others.

You don't have to be forgiven for a skateboard mishap to have a reason to forgive others. Children of God *always* have a reason. Read another story, *The Unkind Friend,* to see how this works.

The Unkind Friend

Katie arrived at school and started looking around for her friends. There was one—Amber! She was talking and laughing with some of the more popular girls.

Katie walked up.
Amber hadn't noticed her yet.

Really, Katie is such a loser. I don't know why I act like she's my friend.

Oh—Katie. Um...I didn't see you.

Wh...What did you say?

Come on girls, let's go. We don't have to talk to this loser.

Katie and Amber didn't speak the rest of the day. Katie was hurt . . . and mad! She started thinking of ways she could make *everyone* hate Amber. A few times when she looked at Amber, Amber looked the other way. Katie thought her used-to-be friend might have been feeling guilty, but not really sorry.

"ONE WEEK LATER"

A week went by. Katie wished she could heal her conflict with Amber. She knew it meant she had to forgive Amber—even though Amber didn't deserve it and hadn't even asked! So Katie prayed.

Father, help me to stop counting Amber's mean words against her. Help me to stop hating her for what she did.

Katie also knew she had said mean things herself sometimes. God had forgiven her for those words—and much more. Katie thanked God that he forgave her for *so much*. He forgave her for *every* sin she'd *ever* done!

Thank you, Father, for forgiving me so completely.

The next day Katie saw Amber at school. She knew she might never be able to fully trust Amber again. But she still wanted to heal their conflict and start wishing good things for Amber.

Amber, can we talk?

What might Katie say? Fill in what you think she might tell Amber.

TALK ABOUT IT

Share what you wrote for Katie to say. Do you think the way Katie knew and treasured God's forgiveness should make her MORE LIKELY or LESS LIKELY to be able to forgive Amber?

Like Katie, you need to truly treasure the forgiveness you've received from God and know how BIG it is. It's much bigger than the forgiveness Ethan got from Mrs. Vincent. It lets you forgive even very hurtful sins like what Amber did to Katie.

PART 2: HOW MUCH SHOULD I FORGIVE?

If *your* forgiveness is based on God's forgiveness of you, that helps you know how much you should forgive others. Fill in the blanks to tell how big God's forgiveness is, looking up Bible verses to help.

God forgives me OF EVERYTHING. He cleanses me from

_____(1 John 1:9).

God forgives me COMPLETELY, AS MUCH AS HE CAN. He removes my sins from me as far as

_____ (Psalm 103:12).

God forgives me WITHOUT KEEPING A RECORD OF HOW BAD I WAS.

He _____, nailing it to the cross (Colossians 2:14).

Forgiveness is always costly to the person who forgives.

When the master in Jesus's story forgave his servant, it cost him much money.

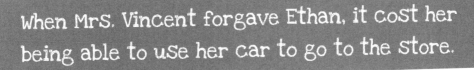

When Mrs. Vincent forgave Ethan, it cost her being able to use her car to go to the store.

When Katie forgave Amber, it cost her the chance to get even for how she'd been hurt.

God forgives me WITH THE MOST COSTLY PAYMENT OF ALL. Jesus ransomed me (bought me back) not with silver or gold, but with

_____ (1 Peter 1:18–19).

Just like there's false repentance, there can be FAKE FORGIVENESS. It usually involves saying, "I'll only forgive you if . . ." It means you still want the other person to pay somehow instead of accepting the cost of forgiveness yourself.

Look at some of the ways Katie might have "forgiven" Amber.

FAKE FORGIVENESS #1:

"I'll forgive you this one time. But you better not say mean things about me again."

FAKE FORGIVENESS #2:

"I'll only forgive you if you're really sorry. That's for your own good, you know."

FAKE FORGIVENESS #3:

"If you do something for me to make up for what you did, then maybe I'll forgive you. Otherwise I'd just be letting you get away with being mean."

FAKE FORGIVENESS #4:

"I forgive you. But you should know I'm only doing it because I'm a Christian and I have to."

Now match each kind of fake forgiveness with how Katie still wanted Amber to pay. Put the number from the fake forgiveness above next to the attitude below that fits it.

_____ "You have to pay by feeling bad."

_____ "You have to pay by knowing I'm still mad at you."

_____ "You have to pay by paying me back."

_____ "You have to pay by never sinning against me again."

TALK ABOUT IT

Do any of these kinds of fake forgiveness sometimes seem right to you? Which ones? Why? Discuss how they might just be ways to make the other person pay?

It's easy to think of reasons to limit your forgiveness. The disciple Peter once asked Jesus, "Lord, how often should I forgive someone who sins against me? Seven times?" (Matthew 18:21 NLT). Peter wanted to put a reasonable limit on how much he had to forgive.

"No, not seven times," Jesus replied, "but seventy times seven!" (v. 22 NLT).

Can you do that math? 70 x 7 = _____ times.

Wow! That's a lot of forgiveness. Jesus says to keep forgiving again and again. Based on what you've learned about forgiveness, check why you think you should not limit how much you forgive.

_____ Because God wants to test you by commanding something really hard.

_____ Because Christians are supposed to let people take advantage of them.

_____ Because God forgives you for the same horrible thing again and again, with no limits.

TALK ABOUT IT

End by talking about a time when someone did wrong to you. Share what happened, or write it or draw a picture of it below. (If you prefer, you can imagine how someone *might* do wrong to you.)

How could you show true forgiveness to that person because Jesus forgave you?
Consider these questions:

❑   What would it cost you to forgive them?

❑   How could you show that you don't count what they did against them anymore?

Discuss your answers with the group, and pray that God would help you to forgive.

MAKE IT STICK:

PICK A FAVORITE THING YOU'VE LEARNED

INSTRUCTIONS:

- ❏ Fill out this Make It Stick page during the week.
- ❏ Don't forget to bring your *Student Guide* back next time you meet.
- ❏ If you have time, go ahead and get started now.

There's just one more lesson left. Before the last lesson, think back through all the lessons and pick something that really impressed you. Do you have a favorite part?

(HINT: If you can, you might want to look back though your lessons or your Make It Stick pages to remind yourself of what you've done. Otherwise, just see what you can remember.)

Once you pick something, write it in the space below or draw a picture that makes you think of it. Be ready to tell what was the BEST THING you learned.

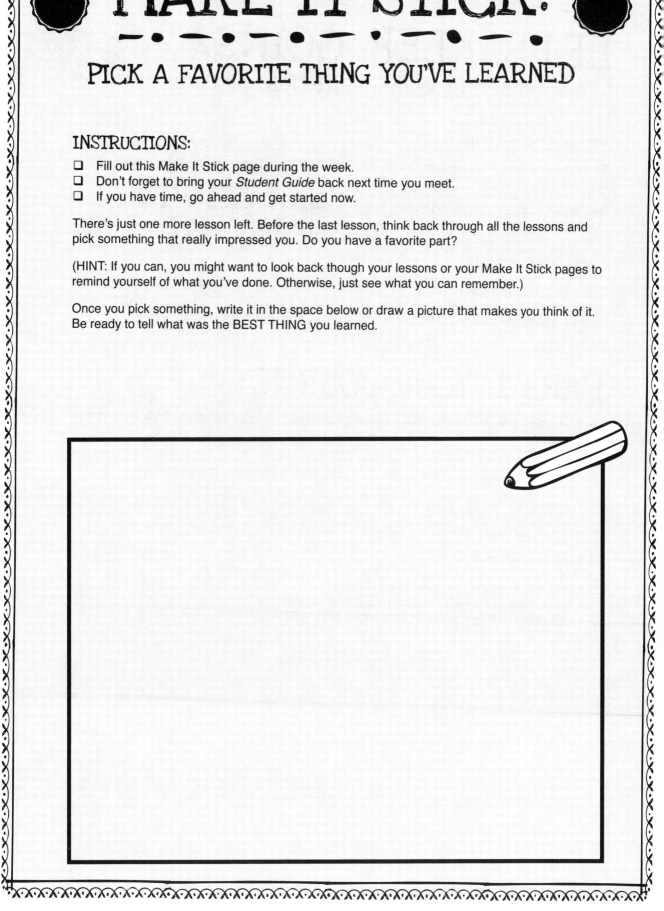

LET'S. KEEP. GOING.

Big Idea: A Lifetime of Faith

BEFORE YOU BEGIN

Share the best thing you've learned so far from *What's Up?* Can you see any change in your life from what you've learned? Give an example.

Pray together. Thank God for what each person has learned and how they've grown in Jesus. Ask him to keep working in you.

TODAY'S LESSON

This lesson will look back at much of what you've already learned and review it. It'll also look ahead at how you can *use* what you've learned for the rest of your life. Think of it as a road trip. There are places you've been and places you're going. We'll call it "the journey of faith."

PART 1: YOUR JOURNEY

Much of what you've learned in *What's Up?* could be summed up by **Galatians 2:20**. Look up that verse and fill in the blank to complete the statement below.

I live _____ in the Son of God, who loved me and gave himself for me.

Your life is a journey of faith. Faith means believing in Jesus and trusting him. You need to . . .

- ❏ Believe God's promises
- ❏ Believe God loves and accepts you (because you're joined to Jesus)
- ❏ Believe God forgives you (because of Jesus)
- ❏ Believe God welcomes you as his child (because of Jesus)
- ❏ Believe you're holy in Jesus and becoming even more holy

TALK ABOUT IT

Look at the Journey of Faith figure. Imagine the road trip represents the rest of your life. Along the way, you'll have many choices. You can choose to "drive" with *unbelief* or with *belief*.

Talk about the "cities" along the way. Each stands for a way of *unbelief* or *belief*. Which do you think you've learned the most about? Where have you grown in faith? Where do you most still need to grow?

Point to remember:
You don't have to try hard to have extra strong faith.
What matters is that your faith is in an extra strong person—Jesus!

	WELCOME TO IDOLOPOLIS	WELCOME TO ORPHANTOWN	WELCOME TO REPENTANCE CITY	WELCOME TO CROSSVILLE
Unbelief When I am full of doubt . . .	**My idols control me.** They're like the shark (Lesson 9).	**I depend on myself** like the orphan in Lesson 10.	**My repentance is false.** I'm sorry for what happened to me (Lesson 12).	**I make excuses for my sin.** I don't think about Jesus much (Lesson 7).
Belief When I have faith in Jesus. . .	**God is in charge of my life.** The shark is being killed.	**I depend on my Father** like a son or daughter.	**My repentance is godly.** I am sorry for sinning against God (Lesson 13).	**I admit my sin and trust Jesus for forgiveness.** My trust in Jesus and love for him grows.

PART 2: ABRAHAM, MAN OF FAITH

Now let's look at how the journey of faith worked in the life of Abraham. Of course, Abraham never studied *What's Up?*, but the Bible shows us that he learned all those lessons.

REVIEW

Several lessons ago, you studied a time when Abraham (he was called Abram at the time) failed to live by faith. Remember when he went to Egypt . . .

Abraham didn't believe God would bless him like he promised.

SO . . .

Abraham gave in to the idol of fear that he might be killed.

SO . . .

Abraham lied about his wife, Sarah.

Later in Abraham's life, his faith grew stronger. God also gave him a son, Isaac. That started to fulfill one of the big promises God had made—that through Isaac, Abraham would have many descendants (great-great-grandchildren). Isaac gave Abraham and Sarah much joy!

But read what happened when Isaac was partly grown:

> *After these things God tested Abraham and said to him, "Abraham!" And he said, "Here I am." He said, "Take your son, your only son Isaac, whom you love, and go to the land of Moriah, and offer him there as a burnt offering on one of the mountains of which I shall tell you." (Genesis 22:1–2)*

DIRECTIONS:

Find the word "tested" and circle it. God was testing Abraham's faith. It would take faith for Abraham to do what God said.

Also find the words "burnt offering" and circle them. A burnt offering was a sacrifice to pay for sin. God told Abraham to kill Isaac to pay for sin. What a horrible price to pay!

When God told Abraham to sacrifice Isaac, what idols do you think Abraham might have had in his life that tempted him not to obey that command? Think of a few (you don't have to fill in all the blanks).

What might Abraham have LOVED more than he loved God?

_____

_____

_____

_____

What might Abraham have TRUSTED more than he trusted God?

_____

_____

_____

What might Abraham have FEARED that came before God?

_____

_____

To pass the test, Abraham had to <u>believe</u> God would still keep his promises, make him happy and completely bless him—even if Isaac were killed. In fact, Abraham <u>did believe</u> something huge about God. **Read Hebrews 11:17–19** to see what Abraham believed.

Abraham believed that God was able to _____.

WELCOME TO ORPHANTOWN

Abraham also had to <u>believe</u> that God loved him and was taking care of him like a Father. For each pair below . . .

❑ Cross out the orphan thinking that would have led Abraham to disobey God.

❑ Circle the thinking like a son that Abraham needed in order to obey God.

Finally, decide which example of orphan thinking would have been most tempting.

"I just CAN'T fail with Isaac. It's up to me to make sure nothing bad happens to him."

"It's okay for me to be weak and trust God. He has a good plan even if something happens to Isaac."

"Isaac finally made me into a person who's worth something— a father! I'll be worthless again without him."

"My worth as a person comes from belonging to God. Not even losing Isaac can take that away from me."

"I've been trying hard to obey God and he should have noticed how good I've been. It isn't fair that he's making me do this!"

"God counts me righteous because I believe, not because of how good I can be. He always gives me more than I deserve."

"Even if I don't have Isaac, I still have so very much love from God."

"If I don't have Isaac, I've lost everything!"

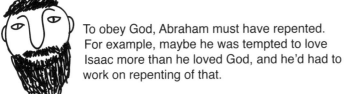

To obey God, Abraham must have repented. For example, maybe he was tempted to love Isaac more than he loved God, and he'd had to work on repenting of that.

Think of some of the excuses and false obedience (obeying with a selfish attitude) Abraham could have tried. Put a star by the ones that sound like something you'd be tempted to try.

"I'm not sure I understood you right, God, so I'm going to hold off on this. See, I'm trying to be obedient. I don't want to make a mistake with something so important."

"What you said isn't fair, God. I deserve better. You need to consider that."

"Okay, I'll do it. But how soon do I have to start? Do I have to do it NOW?"

"If I do this, I hope you don't expect me to like you anymore—because I won't."

"I guess I have to do this because you're God, and if I don't you can make my life terrible. So I will."

Abraham didn't try any of these. Instead, the Bible says he saddled his donkey early the next morning and left with Isaac to sacrifice him at Moriah. Along the way he said good things about God's care, not bad things. Discuss what you think Abraham must have <u>believed</u> in order to have such true obedience and repentance.

WELCOME TO
CROSSVILLE
✝

Finally, Abraham had to <u>believe</u> that he was a big sinner, but God would find a way to pay for his sin. Abraham lived many years before Jesus. He didn't know about the cross. But he still believed that God himself would be the one to pay for sin.

God had said Isaac would be the burnt offering. But Abraham believed God actually had a better plan. Read what happened as he and Isaac climbed the mountain at Moriah, and <u>underline</u> what Abraham said God would do.

Isaac said to his father Abraham, "My father!" And he said, "Here I am, my son." He said, "Behold, the fire and the wood, but where is the lamb for a burnt offering?" Abraham said, "God will provide for himself the lamb for a burnt offering, my son." (Genesis 22:7–8)

Sure enough, after Abraham passed the faith test and was ready to sacrifice Isaac, God called to him to stop. He provided a ram instead. Abraham and Isaac sacrificed it and worshiped God.

Years later, God provided the only sacrifice that really paid for all of Abraham's sin and for the sin of everyone else who has faith. Jesus died on the cross. He's the sacrifice that pays for your sin—ALL OF IT, no matter how bad you've been!

Circle the statement that best fits Abraham's approach to his sin.

EXCUSES: "God, most of my sin was stuff I couldn't help. It isn't fair that you ask me to sacrifice Isaac for it."

PRETENDING: "I don't sin that much. I'm really pretty good. Let me show you that the payment you demand is too steep."

ADMITTING (AND FAITH): "Yes, I'm a horrible sinner. I deserve to pay a horrible price for my sin. But I'm trusting that you will pay that horrible price instead."

Which way of thinking will make Abraham love God more? Which will make him obey better? Discuss why.

PART 3: WHO YOU ARE

The lessons you've studied are about WHO YOU ARE if you believe. You're a person joined to Jesus, who died on the cross and rose to life for you. It makes you a son or daughter of God, because you're joined to *the* Son of God. Read what the Bible says about that:

> *You are all sons of God through faith in Christ Jesus, for all of you who were baptized into*
>
> *Christ have clothed yourselves with Christ. (Galatians 3:26–27 NIV)*

UNDERLINE the part that connects faith in Jesus with being a son.

DOUBLE UNDERLINE the part that says it's like wearing Jesus as your clothes.

That's a strange picture, isn't it—"clothed with Christ"? Try to draw that picture. In the space below, draw yourself wearing a long, white robe. Make sure the robe in your picture covers all your other clothes.

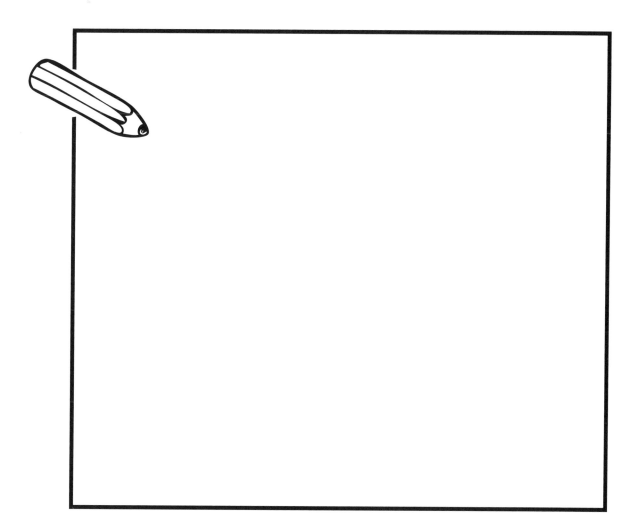

Now write "JESUS" on the robe. That's your picture of you being clothed with Christ.

THINK ABOUT CLOTHES.

You'd be ASHAMED if you were wearing no clothes. You might also feel embarrassed if you were wearing really cheap or ugly or dorky clothes.

And you might feel PROUD and better than others if you were wearing really expensive or pretty or extra cool clothes.

Well, it's easy to feel the same about what others think of you. You might be ASHAMED and try to cover up what's wrong with you if others:

❑ Think you're stupid.

❑ Catch you doing something wrong.

❑ Find out you're really pretty uncool.

❑ Notice a mistake you made.

❑ See your sin.

❑ Scold you or make fun of you.

(Put an X by one or two that might make you feel especially ashamed.)

Or you might feel PROUD and better than others if people:

❑ Think you're smart.

❑ Notice you doing something right.

❑ Never catch you making mistakes.

❑ See your good behavior.

❑ Praise you and reward you.

(Put a ★STAR by some that make you feel proud and better than others.)

But if you're clothed in Jesus, all those things are like the clothes underneath your big robe. Who cares? They don't matter; Jesus matters instead.

Jesus forgives what's wrong with you. Jesus also gives you a righteousness that's better than anything that's right with you. Those other things can't make you ashamed or proud any more. What people think of you doesn't make who you are. *A person who's in Jesus* is who you are!

TALK ABOUT IT

Discuss the things you put an X or a star ★ by. How would they stop mattering to you if you believed more fully that you're a son or daughter, clothed in Jesus?

CONCLUSION

Now turn all the way back to Lesson 1 where you picked a word or short phrase that best fit the way you thought about Christianity when you began *What's Up?*. Copy what you wrote here:

"Christianity is _____."

Has your thinking changed because of what you've studied since then? If it has, pick a new word now to describe how you think now:

"Now Christianity seems to me to be all about _____."

Share the word you picked. Discuss what you learned that made it change.

PRAY ABOUT IT

God can help *you* live by faith, just like Abraham did. Use Philippians 1:6 as the theme for your closing prayer. It says:

"I am sure of this, that he who began a good work in you will bring it to completion at the day of Jesus Christ."

Pray that God would keep up the good work he's begun in you. Ask him to teach you more of his great love for you and help you to believe it more deeply.

mission
grace through you

At Serge we believe that mission begins through the gospel of Jesus Christ bringing God's grace into the lives of believers. It also sustains us and empowers us to go into different cultures bringing the good news of forgiveness of sins and new life to those whom God is calling to himself.

As a cross-denominational, reformed, sending agency with 200 missionaries on over 25 teams in 5 continents, we are always looking for people who are ready to take the next step in sharing Christ, through:

- **Short-term Teams:** One to two-week trips oriented around serving overseas ministries while equipping the local church for mission

- **Internships:** Eight-week to nine-month opportunities to learn about missions through serving with our overseas ministry teams

- **Apprenticeships:** Intensive 12–24 month training and ministry opportunities for those discerning their call to cross-cultural ministry

- **Career:** One- to five-year appointments designed to nurture you for a lifetime of ministry

Serge Grace at the Fray   Visit us online at: www.serge.org/mission